# MIRRORS FOR BEHAVIOR

AN ANTHOLOGY OF CLASSROOM OBSERVATION INSTRUMENTS

# MIRRORS FOR BEHAVIOR

## AN ANTHOLOGY OF CLASSROOM OBSERVATION INSTRUMENTS

EDITED BY:

ANITA SIMON

E. GIL BOYER

TECHNICAL ASSISTANCE

GERTRUDE MOSKOWITZ

RESEARCH FOR BETTER SCHOOLS, INC.

A REGIONAL EDUCATION LABORATORY

AND

THE CENTER FOR THE STUDY OF TEACHING

TEMPLE UNIVERSiTY

Distributed by

Research for Better Schools, Inc., Philadelphia, Pennsylvania
Under the Provisions of Title IV ESEA of 1965 in cooperation
with the USOE,
Under Research Contract #O.E.C. 1-7-062867-3053 -
A Regional Educational Laboratory

Library of Congress Catalog Card Number: 67-31735

# FOREWORD

Many times problems which initially appear to be simple in nature and hold promise for quick solutions end up with complexities far beyond the anticipated simplicity. Such was our recent experience.

E. Gil Boyer, Director of Research for Research for Better Schools, was charged with the mission of evaluating teacher behavior in one of our major projects, "Individually Prescribed Instruction." At the same time, the staff of the College of Education at Temple University was in the process of creating the Center for the Study of Teaching.

A mutual interest in the application of classroom observation systems to Individually Prescribed Instruction was encouraged by Leon Ovsiew, Assistant Dean for the College of Education at Temple University. The results of this encouragement led to cooperation between RBS and the Center for the Study of Teaching.

Anita Simon, of Temple University, with E. Gil Boyer of RBS, became the principal participants using a modified Flanders instrument to study teacher behavior in the classroom setting of Individually Prescribed Instruction. The results gathered from the modified instrument left both investigators with many unanswered questions.

While seeking answers, it became apparent to Simon and Boyer that "interaction analysis instruments" had considerable potential for developing effective "humanizing" curricula for children. Indeed, the instruments held promise for both paper-pencil content and computer mediated content in a mode the same as that of Individually Prescribed Instruction.

Then came the complexities. Armed with a hypothesis of "considerable potential," the investigators collected the major existing classroom observation instruments. The results of their labor, too numerous to trace, are presented in this anthology, Mirrors for Behavior.

Since interest in the area of classroom observation has been exhibited by three-fourths of the regional educational laboratories, Research for Better Schools decided to share their findings. The limited edition contains not only the anthology but copies of the actual systems and publications of the various inventors and authors as well. It is being made available to the other regional educational laboratories with the express hope of providing additional information.

The Classroom Interaction Newsletter, edited by Simon, will publish a condensation of the systems as a special edition for its subscribers, thus making available copies to libraries and qualified researchers at cost.

*James W. Becker*
Executive Director
Research for Better Schools, Inc.

November 30, 1967

i

## PREFACE

Classroom interaction analysis systems are a relatively new data collection technique. The lengthy bibliographical section of this volume is an indication of the rapidly growing interest of the educational researcher and not the antiquity of the technique. This volume contains an overview of the field, a synthesis of the developments to date, a prognosis of future use, an annotated compilation of twenty-six instruments representing a variety of approaches both in the affective and cognitive domains, and an extensive bibliography of reports of research and teacher training activities using classroom observation instruments.

It should be noted that this collection is not intended as a book of readings, but rather as a reference for the researcher and student concerned with the development and application of these instruments.

Much of the work reported here has not appeared in print before and it is hoped that this collection will supply a missing communication link among the developers and potential users of these systems.

*Anita Simon*
*E. Gil Boyer*

## ACKNOWLEDGMENTS

We wish to express our appreciation to the authors of the systems and their publishers for the generous cooperation which made this collection possible, and to extend our apologies for the considerable intrusion into their busy schedules.

We further wish to acknowledge the contributions of the staff of Research for Better Schools and of Russell Hill, Director of the Center for the Study of Teaching and his staff, without which this collection could not have been made. Special appreciation is extended to Gertrude Moskowitz, who collected a major portion of the technical data about these systems directly from their authors, Bruce Yasgur and Ethel Goldberg who tracked down the endless changes and permissions, Yvonne Agazarian for her organizational recommendations, Joan Weiner who typed the many drafts of the manuscript; and Michele Shapiro for the reformatting of the many and varied bibliographical references.

# Table of Contents

Page

FOREWORD . . . . . . . . . . . . . . . . . . . . . . . . . . . . . . . . . . . . . . . . . . . . . . . . . . . . . . .   i

PREFACE. . . . . . . . . . . . . . . . . . . . . . . . . . . . . . . . . . . . . . . . . . . . . . . . . . . . . .   iii

## Section One

MIRRORS FOR BEHAVIOR . . . . . . . . . . . . . . . . . . . . . . . . . . . . . . . . . . .   1

Overview . . . . . . . . . . . . . . . . . . . . . . . . . . . . . . . . . . . . . . . . . . . . . . . . . . . . . .   1

> The two dozen-plus classroom observation systems in this
> anthology were primarily designed to collect data about pupil
> and teacher behaviors.  The focus of the systems varies with
> the interest of their authors.

The Affective Systems . . . . . . . . . . . . . . . . . . . . . . . . . . . . . . . . . . . . . . . . . .   3

> The affective systems deal with the emotional climate of the
> classroom and how it is conditioned by teacher reactions to
> pupils' feelings, ideas, work efforts, or actions.

The Cognitive Systems . . . . . . . . . . . . . . . . . . . . . . . . . . . . . . . . . . . . . . . . . .   7

> The cognitive systems deal with two aspects of cognition:  the
> thinking process itself and the verbal patterns used to deal
> with them.

Coding and Data Reduction. . . . . . . . . . . . . . . . . . . . . . . . . . . . . . . . . . . . . .   12

> A brief summary of the coding techniques used to gather data
> about teacher and pupil behaviors and to reduce the data to
> formats for "feedback" and research analysis.

Uses . . . . . . . . . . . . . . . . . . . . . . . . . . . . . . . . . . . . . . . . . . . . . . . . . . . . . . . . .   16

> To date, classroom observation instruments have been used
> primarily in three ways:
>
> Research - To describe what goes on in the classroom, to
> build theoretical models, and to relate the process of teach-
> ing to cognitive growth and behavioral changes in pupils.
>
> Teacher Training - These instruments are enjoying an in-
> creasing role in both expanding the repertoire of teaching
> styles, and providing teachers with objective data about how
> their teaching styles match their intent.
>
> Supervision - These instruments are changing the supervisor's
> role from rater to resource by providing them with a tool to
> help teachers become effective self-evaluators of their own
> teaching skills.

The Future .................................................................... 22

Verbal interaction systems can be modified for use as curriculum content designed to help pupils learn how to solve problems, make decisions and communicate effectively.

## Section Two

### ANTHOLOGY OF CLASSROOM OBSERVATION INSTRUMENTS

These systems are individually paginated and appear in the following order:

1. Amidon System (MCS)
2. Amidon-Hunter System (VICS)
3. Aschner-Gallagher System
4. Bellack System
5. Flanders System
6. Flanders System (Sub-categories)
7. Gallagher System
8. Honigman System (MACI)
9. Hough System
10. Hughes System
11. Joyce System
12. Lindvall System
13. Medley System (OScAR 4V)
14. Miller System
15. Moskowitz System (FLint)
16. Oliver-Shaver System
17. Openshaw-Cyphert System
18. Simon-Agazarian System (SAVI)
19. Smith System (Logic)
20. Smith System (Strategies)
21. Spaulding System (CASES)
22. Spaulding System (STARS)
23. Taba System
24. Withall System
25. Wright System
26. Wright-Proctor System

## Section Three

### BIBLIOGRAPHY ............................................ B-1

Including most of the reports to date, both published and unpublished, dealing with research and teacher training projects utilizing classroom observation systems.

### INDEX TO SYSTEMS AND AUTHORS BY SYSTEM NUMBERS.. I-1

# Tables

Page

Table I     The Focus of Classroom Interaction Systems ········· 2

There are nine systems dealing with the affective domain,
six systems dealing with the cognitive domain, and ten
systems dealing with both. Five code teacher behaviors
only, two code students only, and the rest deal with both
teacher and student.

Table II     Data Collection Methods Reported ········· 14

Nine of the systems require audio or video tape and seven
of them are sufficiently complex to require more than one
person to administer.

Table III     Uses Reported by Authors ········· 17

All of the systems were designed for and have been used
for research. A dozen of them have been used for teacher
training and nine for supervision.

# Figures

Figure 1     Families of Related Systems ········· 3

There are three general "families of related systems."
They consist of two major subsets in the affective domain;
two more in the cognitive domain; and three composite
systems including the new generalized category system
for both the affective and cognitive domain reported in
this volume.

Figure 2     Generalized Category System: Affective Domain ········· 4

A simplified system for coding teacher reaction to pupils'
ideas, feelings, attempts to set own work standards and
behaviors.

Figure 3     Generalized Category System: Cognitive Domain ········· 10

A simplified system for grouping the cognitive dimensions
into data recall, data processing and evaluation. The system also treats the verbal behavior categories as a separate entity.

Figure 4     Sample Matrix (Flanders) ········· 15

A technique for pairing sequential sets of behaviors and
summarizing data for analysis.

Section One

MIRRORS FOR BEHAVIOR

# MIRRORS FOR BEHAVIOR

Interaction analysis systems are "shorthand" methods for collecting observable objective data about the way people talk and act. They make possible a relatively simple record of what is happening but they do not record what is being said. This anthology contains twenty-six such systems of the fifty-plus that have been developed to date. They differ from each other in a variety of ways, but all of them code some aspect of behavior. These systems are made up of sets of categories of behaviors. Typical categories are lecturing, giving opinions, asking questions, criticizing and praising. Most of these systems are "content free," that is, they can be used with any subject matter or grade level. They are concerned with how teaching and learning takes place.

All of these systems were originally designed for research purposes but they have since found their way into teacher training and supervision. They also have considerable potential for "pupil training" - potential which is the editors' main interest in this collection.

## OVERVIEW

Classroom verbal interaction is a complex process and no one category system measures all of the important aspects of teacher-pupil interaction. Each system represents those dimensions which are important to the person who created the system.

There are, however, two major aspects which are of importance to the majority of the people who are observing the classroom scene. These are the "affective" and "cognitive" domains. Some systems focus exclusively on one domain or the other, and some on both. The literature provides, however, no consensus about criteria for deciding in which domain a system belongs. For the purposes of this anthology we have designated the systems as affective, cognitive or both in the following manner:

The affective systems deal with the emotional climate of the classroom by coding how the teacher reacts to the feelings, ideas, work efforts or actions of the pupil. The way the teacher responds to pupils determines, in large measure, the affective climate of the classroom. Therefore, we have placed categories that measure teachers' reactions to a variety of pupil responses in the affective domain.

The cognitive systems, on the other hand, deal with the thinking process itself. The cognitive systems consist of categories which differentiate between different kinds of teacher information, teacher questions, or pupil responses. Most of the systems which focus primarily or totally on the cognitive area have complex coding procedures requiring equally complex collection schemes such as tape recording transcripts. Of course, every statement carries both a data and an emotional message, and in reality these are probably not separable. However, if the system is primarily concerned with measuring the emotional climate of the classroom, it is considered affective and if it is primarily concerned with thought processes, it is considered cognitive. (See Table I)

Table I

## THE FOCUS OF CLASSROOM INTERACTION SYSTEMS

| SYSTEM | SYSTEM FOCUS | | | | TYPE OF COMMUNICATION RECORDED | | SUBJECT OF OBSERVATION | | |
|---|---|---|---|---|---|---|---|---|---|
| | Affective domain | Cognitive domain | Work process (control) | Behavior | Verbal | Nonverbal | Teacher only | Student only | Teacher and student |
| 1. AMIDON | X | X | | | X | | | | X |
| 2. AMIDON-HUNTER (VICS) | X | | | | X | | | | X |
| 3. ASCHNER-GALLAGHER | | X | | | X | X | | | X |
| 4. BELLACK | | X | | | X | | | | X |
| 5. FLANDERS | X | | | | X | | | | X |
| 6. FLANDERS (Expanded) | X | | | | X | | | | X |
| 7. GALLAGHER | | X | | | X | | | | X |
| 8. HONIGMAN (MACI) | X | | X | X | X | X | | | X |
| 9. HOUGH | X | | | | X | | | | X |
| 10. HUGHES | X | | | | X | X | | | X |
| 11. JOYCE | X | X | X | | X | | X | | |
| 12. LINDVALL | | | | X | | X | | X | |
| 13. MEDLEY (OScAR) | X | X | X | | X | | | | X |
| 14. MILLER | X | | | | X | | X | | |
| 15. MOSKOWITZ (FLint) | X | | | | X | | | | X |
| 16. OLIVER-SHAVER | | X | X | | X | | | | X |
| 17. OPENSHAW-CYPHERT | X | X | X | | X | X | X | | |
| 18. SIMON-AGAZARIAN (SAVI) | X | X | | | X | | | | X |
| 19. SMITH (Logic) | | X | | | X | | | | X |
| 20. SMITH (Strategy) | | X | | | X | | | | X |
| 21. SPAULDING (CASES) | X | | | X | X | X | | X | |
| 22. SPAULDING (STARS) | X | X | X | X | X | X | X | | |
| 23. TABA | X | X | | | X | | | | X |
| 24. WITHALL | X | X | | | X | | X | | |
| 25. WRIGHT | X | X | | | X | | | | X |
| 26. WRIGHT-PROCTOR | X | X | | | X | | | | X |

# THE AFFECTIVE SYSTEMS

The most powerful influence on the direction of the development of category systems which measure the affective climate of the classroom has been the work of H. H. Anderson.

Testing the assumption that the teacher is the single most influential agent in setting classroom climate, Anderson created and used a category system which revealed that the way teachers behave in the classroom does affect the way pupils behave. Teachers who behave in an integrative (supportive fashion) tend to have students who behave integratively, and conversely, dominative teachers have students who are dominative, aggressive, and non-sharing.

Anderson polarized teacher behaviors into dominative versus integrative behaviors, and this concept has influenced the work of Withall, Joyce, Flanders, and the many others who followed in the Flanders' lineage. (See Figure 1)

## Figure 1

### FAMILIES OF RELATED SYSTEMS

AFFECTIVE SYSTEMS

Harold H. Anderson                    Marie Hughes

    Withall                                    Miller

    Flanders

        Amidon (MCS)
        Amidon and Hunter (VICS)
        Flanders, Expanded Category System
        Honigman (MACI)
        Hough
        Moskowitz (FLint)
        Spaulding (CASES)
        Wright (Pupil Involvement)

    Joyce

COGNITIVE SYSTEMS

B. Othanel Smith (Logic)              Muriel Wright and Virginia Proctor

    Smith (Strategies)                    Wright (Cognitive)

    Bellack

COMPOSITE SYSTEMS

Modified Category System (MCS) Amidon

Taxonomy of Teacher Behaviors, Openshaw and Cyphert

Generalized Category System (GCS), Simon and Boyer

3

An analysis of the affective categories of the twenty-six category systems included in this volume suggests that there are four dimensions into which this domain can be subdivided. All of the affective categories fit into one or another of these four dimensions. These dimensions consist entirely of categories which comprise teacher reactions to various kinds of pupil verbal or nonverbal "outputs" or behaviors.

The four dimensions are:

1) Teacher reactions to pupils' ideas or cognitive output.

2) Teacher reactions to pupils' feelings or emotional output.

3) Teacher reactions to pupils' attempts to manage classroom procedure and set standards.

4) Teacher reactions to pupils' nonverbal behaviors.

The teacher responses to these four dimensions of the affective domain can range along a continuum from rejecting to accepting, with a variety of interim responses including such categories as praising, neutrally accepting, ignoring, or rejecting pupil output in any of the four dimensions. A generalized affective category system is shown in Figure two.

Figure 2

GENERALIZED CATEGORY SYSTEM: AFFECTIVE DOMAIN

| PUPIL OUTPUT | TEACHER REACTION | |
| --- | --- | --- |
| | Negative ← | → Positive |
| 0  Unspecified | Non-specific criticism or blame | Non-specific praise |
| 1  Ideas | Ignores or rejects student's ideas | Accepts student's ideas |
| 2  Feelings | Ignores or rejects student's feelings | Accepts student's feelings |
| 3  Procedural | Rejects pupil attempts to set own standards and create own working procedures | Shares or encourages responsibility for setting own standards and creating own working procedures |
| 4  Behavior | Limits or criticizes behavior | Accepts or ignores deviate behavior |

The affective domain assesses how the teacher reinforces the pupil and which of the four dimensions of pupil output he chooses to emphasize.

Most of the category systems have some generalized measure of teacher approval and disapproval. Many provide a way of determining if the teacher is accepting student feelings as contrasted with accepting his ideas, but generally rejection is not similarly differentiated. Only six systems reflect concern for group process and for the development of student independence, and only two have categories for measuring teacher responses to pupil non-verbal behaviors.

To the extent that the category systems in this volume reflect teacher behaviors which exist in the classrooms in America, there is considerable lack of emphasis on helping pupils to learn how to clarify and use their feelings constructively, to learn how to create efficient work procedures, or to evaluate their own work.

There has been considerable interest, but little speculation and even less research into a curious aspect of these instruments, that is why these measures of the teacher's affective response to pupil outputs predict subsequent pupil cognitive outputs such as achievement in subject matter and even rise in intelligence scores. It is surprising enough when a variable in education actually predicts something, but it is even more surprising to find that how teachers say what they say appears to be a better predictor of change in pupil behavior than anything else educational research has turned up to date.

One reason why the first affective dimension, acceptance or rejection of pupil's ideas, may predict cognitive growth is because these affective measures deal with the reinforcement the child receives for his content handling skills. How the teacher responds to pupil cognitive output is what supplies the student with positive or negative reinforcement. If the student's idea (the content of his message) is accepted by the teacher, the student is positively reinforced. If the teacher responds negatively, or in any way leaves the student in doubt, the student is negatively reinforced, and his "learning" both of how to learn and what to learn, is impaired. In other words, the affective measures of the teacher's verbal reactions deal with the success or failure of the child to get positive "feedback" about the appropriateness of his message. Affective systems deal in large part with the reinforcement climate in which the student exists. This may explain why the use of systems which deal with acceptance or rejection of pupil ideas predict achievement.

The second dimension of the affective domain focuses on teacher acceptance or rejection of pupil's feelings. Although there has been little research done on the effect of accepting pupil's feelings, theoretically teachers' use of this dimension is a potent predictor of pupil achievement. Every statement heard by the student will contain both an "information" message and an "emotional" message as well. For instance, a teacher statement like, "Even a kindergartner knows that Columbus discovered America" will tell a sixth grader who discovered America, but it will probably also tell him that the teacher thinks he is not very bright. For the student, the affective "You're not very bright" part of the message will probably override the data message "Columbus discovered America."

In a sufficiently threatening or ambiguous environment, it appears that the affective portion of the message can so negatively bias the climate that the content portion is not heard at all. How pupil feelings are handled sets this type of climate directly or indirectly and therefore affects his cognitive output. Thus the pupil's ability to deal with content is lessened and can be thought of either as limiting the ability to receive input or as negative reinforcement.

A somewhat similar phenomenon operates in the third dimension of the affective domain, that of classroom management which includes the setting of standards and work procedures. The manner in which a teacher reacts to pupils' efforts to control their own working environment will affect the learning climate.

Three possible reasons come to mind:

1) If the teacher consistently reserves the power to make decisions about procedures and standards, experience in decision-making is denied to the student. It is the denial of this kind of learning that makes it possible to teach democracy at the rote message level and deny its practice.

2) It is entirely possible that autocratic teacher behavior limits resources available because in this type of classroom, the teacher is the only one who can legitimately

provide inputs. Thus, to the extent that he limits student self-control, students not only lose the opportunity to practice behavioral (including cognitive) skills but also lose the considerable cognitive resources of their peers as well.

3) As children get older, response to their peers becomes stronger than response to the teacher. (The older-younger generation clash is well documented.) When the teacher reserves the power to set standards and procedures, he often puts himself at odds with the student-peer power structure, and loses to the student's peers his ability to influence the student. This is particularly apparent in the typical American junior high school.

Control over pupil behavior is the fourth of these affective system dimensions, and appears to be a special, nonverbal subset of this same "control" function.

In short, it appears that a positive emotional environment is a very powerful asset to learning, and positive emotional environments are made by teachers whose reactions are supportive of their students' ideas, feelings, work efforts and behaviors.

## THE COGNITIVE SYSTEMS

There are fewer systems dealing with the cognitive domain and they tend to be more complex. Apparently these cognitive systems deal with verbal behavior in two different ways. First, they note categories of verbal behavior such as giving data, asking for data, clarifying, defining and giving opinions and second, these systems attempt to get at some structured analysis of the thought processes themselves. To do this latter job, it is sometimes necessary to analyze a series of statements in order to determine what thought process is taking place.

Apparently, a thought process dimension is not easy to determine explicitly from any single verbal statement because a verbal category like "explaining" (Bellack), "stating" (Smith Logic) or "description" (SAVI) could be describing a pupil's recall about some subject such as a date in history, the name of a chemical compound and so forth. However, it could also be a part of an analysis statement in which the pupil was processing data or even a part of an evaluation statement where the pupil was giving his reasons for some value judgement.

Because these cognitive systems* appear to deal both with identification and modification of thought processes and with verbal categories for doing so, we have separated processes from categories as follows:

I. Cognitive Processes
    1. data recall
    2. data processing
    3. evaluation.

II. Categories of Verbal Behaviors Used to Describe Teacher and Pupil Talk About Subject Matter.

Data recall is the thinking process most widely solicited by teachers. This process has been made a separate dimension to differentiate it from the presumably more complex data processing dimension. The difference between these two dimensions can be made clearer by considering how a computer works. It is entirely possible to have a computer merely store data and, on command, dump (recall) it in the same form and format in which it was stored. An impressively large amount of the "learning" which goes on in our schools is little more than this. That is, students are required to memorize sets of facts and to repeat these facts on command.

This seems to be materially different from storing data in a computer, programming the computer to process the data by sorting, comparing, doing arithmetical and logical operations and then reporting the data in some new form and order different from that in which the data was originally placed in the machine. This would be analagous to the data processing dimension in the cognitive domain and includes grouping, classifying, labeling, analyzing and so forth. Determining how best to teach students to use these types of thinking processes is one of the major potential uses of these cognitive systems.

Evaluation seems to be a sufficiently different enough thought process to be considered a cognitive dimension of its own. The evaluation dimension includes both opinions and judgements based on some criteria. Analysis of tapescripts of teacher and pupil interaction, where judgements are being made, have led the editors to believe that far too little class-

---

* It should be noted that nearly all systems which are primarily affective in their focus contain categories which differentiate between "broad" and "narrow" student talk. Although this is an indication of different types of cognition, such categories do not supply enough data to determine which dimension of thought processes is involved.

room work in developing and stating criteria for evaluation is being done. These category systems help analyze the process of formulating value judgements, and research in this area should help develop techniques for improving how value judgements are made. Value judgements are always made by reference to some criteria although the criteria are not always stated, and it appears quite frequently that students make judgements without any clear understanding of the criteria they are using. Often the criteria are unstated and perhaps unrecognized feelings about a subject.

We have been able to identify only three criteria used in making judgements. They are public, private and pragmatic.

Public criteria can be considered as the values and laws of the culture such as prudence, economy, justice and simplicity. They appear in the classroom in statements such as, "Don't talk during assembly because the other pupils can't hear."

Private criteria are usually personal opinions or feelings and appear in such statements as "I don't allow gum chewing in my classroom because I think it rude."

Pragmatic criteria are really statements of probability such as, "I think you had better study for your test, Johnny, because the other four times you didn't, you failed."

Quite often a statement carrying a value judgement or opinion appears without any criteria (the "because" part of the message is not given). These are frequently statements that start with "everybody ought" or "you should" without any reason being given for the statement.

It is interesting to note that in this sense, computers do evaluate, but, unlike pupils, are not usually programmed to give unsupported opinions. Their evaluation processing is usually based on probability and their output is usually the statistical probability of a given result for a given action. For instance, a computer might be used to process complex data about the variables to be considered in determining a trajectory required to put a man on the moon. The output would be a recommended trajectory to do the job at a certain level of confidence. This confidence level would be the probability that the recommended trajectory would do the job.

This kind of "pragmatic evaluation" in which students are taught how to determine the probable consequences of a given act before they perform it does not appear to be common in our schools.

Figure three suggests a generalized category system for the cognitive domain along the dimensions discussed above. Specific verbal categories have not been associated with these cognitive dimensions.

Figure 3

GENERALIZED CATEGORY SYSTEM: COGNITIVE DOMAIN

| I | Cognitive Dimensions |
|---|---|
| | 1. Data Recall |
| | 2. Data Processing |
| |       Enumerate, list, collect, read or report data |
| |       Group, classify, synthesize |
| |       Label, define |
| |       Analyze, compare, contrast |
| |       Infer, generalize, hypothesize |
| | 3. Evaluation |
| |     a. No criteria specified |
| |     b. Private criteria specified |
| |     c. Public criteria specified |
| |     d. Pragmatic (probability) criteria specified |
| II | Categories of Verbal Behavior Used to Describe Teacher and Pupil Talk About Subject Matter |
| |     Stating |
| |     Explaining |
| |     Quoting |
| |     Interpreting |
| |     Elaborating |
| |     Inferring |
| |     Opining |
| |     etc. |

It usually takes more than one verbal statement to determine the cognitive dimension involved. In some cases, coding is a sufficiently complex process to require that both tape recordings and tapescripts of the classroom interaction be used for analysis. This is why very few of the cognitive systems can be coded "live" in the classroom.

It seems reasonable to assume that if _how_ a teacher says _what_ he says has an impact on pupil learning as measured by the affective systems, it should also be reasonable that how a teacher asks for or gives data should also make a difference. A teacher who only asks for data recall should have a different impact on students than one who encourages students to process data in a variety of ways. The differences should show up in the decision-making skills of the students. Students who have been encouraged to develop opinions and value judgements based on pragmatic criteria, students who have been encouraged to recognize value judgements based on their own private criteria and students who are given only public criteria for problem solving should be very different from each other. As yet, this hypothesis remains largely untested. Very little research has been done in teaching problem-solving techniques to pupils or in teaching pupils various ways of making value judgements as a basis for making decisions.

Theoretically, at least, it seems reasonable to propose that teacher behaviors can be modified to elicit more efficient thought processes or thinking skills from students. Further, it seems reasonable that teacher verbal behavior carries as a part of its content, "prescriptions" for how to think. This is true whether or not the teacher is explicitly aware of the "prescription" he is giving. A teacher who asks only data recall questions is prescribing a different thought process than one who asks questions requiring pupils to process data. These prescriptions are the "what" of teaching children how to learn. It is possible that these approaches to how to learn are more important than any reordering or restructuring of the curriculum in the classic sense.

In our present culture where new knowledge is being generated at an exponential rate, and where data is becoming obsolete before it can be processed, skills in how to acquire data and how to process data into useful information are rapidly becoming far more important than the "stockpiling" of facts. If today's schools are to prepare today's children for tomorrow's world, they can ill afford to attempt it by only teaching children how to recall yesterday's data.

## CODING AND DATA REDUCTION

Human memory being what it is, all observation systems require some scheme for coding and collecting the information with which they deal. Among them, one of the most widely used, the Flanders system, is also one of the simplest. Flanders simply assigned the numbers 1 to 10 to the types of talk with which he was concerned. These are coded in somewhat of a continuum for 1 "accepts pupil's feelings" through 7 "criticizes pupil" plus 8 and 9 for two types of pupil response, and 10 for silence, confusion or uncodable interaction.

Other systems, dealing with more than one dimension use more than one set of numbers or a combination of numbers, letters and sometimes even plus and minus. For instance, Gallagher uses a three-digit number in which the hundreds position represents one dimension, the tens position, a second, and the units position, a third. Other systems (such as Bellack and Taba) use a numerical system for one dimension and an alphabetic system for another. In the case of Taba, an alphabetic code is used to deal with who is talking and either a numeric or alphabetic code is used to represent the type of talk which is being carried on. Still others use mnemonic abbreviations (Aschner-Gallagher, and SAVI) or add pluses or minuses for the polarity with which they are dealing (Joyce).

These systems range in complexity from the simple coding schemes of Withall and Flanders to as complex a scheme as Bellack's which has up to eight designations for teacher or pupil statements. Coding complexity is one of the reasons why the use of many of these systems has never extended beyond the researcher who developed them. These coding schemes limit the ways data can be collected. For the more simple ones, data can be collected directly in the classroom, live, by a single observer, and if the categories are clear and mutually exclusive they can be coded with considerable observer reliability. Obviously, the degree of complexity and the ease with which categories can be unambiguously and exclusively identified are of real concern to the potential user of these systems.

The frequency of the coding tallies is usually dependent upon a change in what is occurring, such as, "who is talking." But some systems record a time sense by also tallying the interaction at a prespecified rate such as every three seconds. Thus, the coder has to keep track of two sequences simultaneously: time and recordable changes in the interaction pattern. For instance, in the Flanders system, a teacher lecture of some duration would be recorded with a series of 5's, one 5 being recorded for each three second interval of time. A shift to a question would be indicated by the recording of a 4. Thus, at least twenty notations would be made in each minute.

The use of complex systems requires a tape recording and/or tapescript. Some systems, particularly in the cognitive group, require teams of coders in order to attain reliable scores. (See Table II)

Observers are usually trained with recordings which makes it possible to record for a preset time interval, to check for reliability, and to teach the observer by rerunning the same sequence of interactions several times.

Having collected the data the user is faced with the task of reducing it to some usable form. For some systems this implies no more than a frequency count of the types of coded tallies. Other systems look for the relationship between the dimensions being coded, and still others look for the kinds and frequencies of sequential activities. For instance, in the Flanders system (and to some degree, in others in the Flanders' lineage) a series such as "4-8" (teacher question, narrow pupil response) indicates a very different pattern from "5-9" (teacher statement followed by a broad pupil response).

By pairing the ten categories in the Flanders system, it is possible to generate one hundred different behavioral pairs. They would be paired in the following manner:

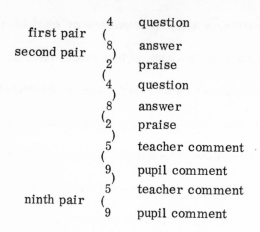

first pair ( 4 question

second pair ( 8 answer / ) 2 praise

( 4 question / ) 8 answer

( 2 praise / ) 5 teacher comment

( 9 pupil comment / ) 5 teacher comment

ninth pair ( 9 pupil comment

By reading down this coded set of observations, a sequential picture of the verbal behaviors becomes obvious. But, for any lengthy observation, or for comparing sets of observations, this can be tedious.

Table II

DATA COLLECTION METHODS REPORTED

| SYSTEM | AUDIO OR VIDEO TAPE REQUIRED | | PERSONNEL NEEDED FOR OBSERVATION OR RECORDING SESSION | | | | NUMBER OF CODERS NEEDED DURING CODING SESSION | | | |
|---|---|---|---|---|---|---|---|---|---|---|
| | No | Yes | 1 coder | Team of 2 | 2 teams of 2 | Tape operator | No coder other than observer(s) | 1 coder | 2 coders | 2 teams of 2 coders |
| 1. AMIDON | X | | X | | | | X | | | |
| 2. AMIDON-HUNTER (VICS) | X | | X | | | | X | | | |
| 3. ASCHNER-GALLAGHER | | X | X | | | X | | | | X |
| 4. BELLACK | | X | | | | X | | | | X |
| 5. FLANDERS | X | | X | | | | X | | | |
| 6. FLANDERS (Expanded) | X | | X | | | | X | | | |
| 7. GALLAGHER | | X | | | | X | | | X | |
| 8. HONIGMAN (MACI) | X | | X | | | | X | | | |
| 9. HOUGH | X | | X | | | | X | | | |
| 10. HUGHES | | X | | X | | X | | | X | |
| 11. JOYCE | X | | X | | | | X | | | |
| 12. LINDVALL | X | | X | | | | X | | | |
| 13. MEDLEY (OScAR) | X | | X | | | | X | | | |
| 14. MILLER | | X | | | | X | | X | | |
| 15. MOSKOWITZ (FLint) | X | | X | | | | X | | | |
| 16. OLIVER-SHAVER | | X | | | | X | | X | | |
| 17. OPENSHAW-CYPHERT | X | | | | X | | X | | | |
| 18. SIMON-AGAZARIAN (SAVI) | X | | X | | | | X | | | |
| 19. SMITH (Logic) | | X | | | | X | | | | X |
| 20. SMITH (Strategy) | | X | | | | X | | | | X |
| 21. SPAULDING (CASES) | X | | X | | | | X | | | |
| 22. SPAULDING (STARS) | X | | X | | | | X | | | |
| 23. TABA | | X | | | | X | | X | | |
| 24. WITHALL | X | | X | | | | X | | | |
| 25. WRIGHT | X | | X | | | | X | | | |
| 26. WRIGHT-PROCTOR | X | | X | | | | X | | | |

By building this sequence into a matrix, a simplified pattern of what is happening emerges. This is done by entering each number into the matrix twice, once as the first number in the pair, and once as the second number in the pair. The resultant build-up in the cells of the matrix helps illuminate the interaction patterns. For instance, in the following sample matrix each pair of numbers is entered along the intersection of the row and

Figure 4

SAMPLE MATRIX (FLANDERS)

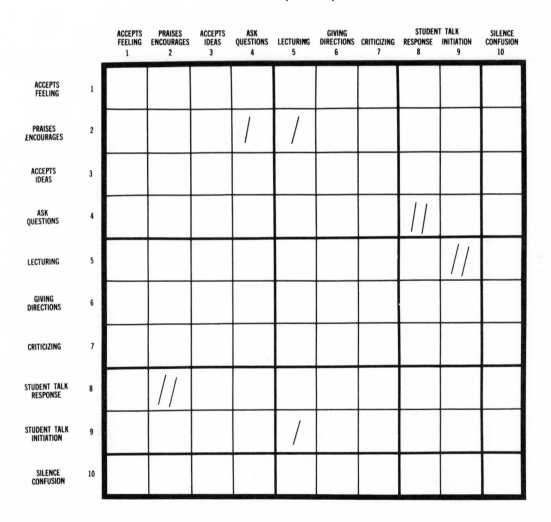

column in row-column order. Thus, the 4-8 shows in the intersection of the fourth row and eight column and the following 8-2 appears in the eight row, second column, followed by the 2-4 in the second row, fourth column, etc. The number of tallies in the intersection of the fourth row and eighth column indicates the frequency with which this teacher asks questions that were responded to by narrow answers, and the build-up in the fifth row, ninth column represents teacher statements followed by a broad student response which indicates a very different (and not very typical) classroom pattern.

This approach to data reduction has been assigned to a variety of computers, including in the IBM area alone, the 7090, 1401 and the 360 series. The computer programs are typically used to build the matrices, to reduce them to percentages and to develop pertinent statistics such as the relationship of criticism to praise, teacher to pupil talk, indirect to direct categories and the like.

To date, only the Flanders, OScAR and the Taba systems have been used widely by other than their designers. Considerable work needs to be done in simplification of the systems, sharpening of category definitions, and facilitating coding techniques and developing methodology for analysis. As sharper identifications are made of the various interactions these systems attempt to measure, it will be possible to extend their use. The growing availability of both audio and video tapes should also play a considerable role in the expansion of their use. It is hoped that this collection, the first of its kind in the field, will encourage developments which will make these systems more usable in improving education.

## USES

The proliferation of classroom observation systems appears to be due to their fulfilling a function vital to both educational research and to teacher training. They provide the objective data necessary for research, teacher training and supervision. Table III indicates the uses of these systems reported by their authors.

Prior to the 1960's, almost all research on "effective teaching" concentrated on seeking links between characteristics of teachers or of teaching settings (input) and various kinds

16

of pupil growth (output).* Inclusion of process measures of teacher behavior in studies of teacher effectiveness has constituted a major change in research in this field. Data from

## Table III
## USES REPORTED BY AUTHOR

| SYSTEM | Research | Teacher Training | Supervision | SYSTEM | Research | Teacher Training | Supervision |
|--------|----------|------------------|-------------|--------|----------|------------------|-------------|
| 1. AMIDON | X | | | 14. MILLER | X | X | X |
| 2. AMIDON-HUNTER (VICS) | X | X | X | 15. MOSKOWITZ (FLint) | X | X | |
| 3. ASCHNER-GALLAGHER | X | | | 16. OLIVER-SHAVER | X | | |
| 4. BELLACK | X | | | 17. OPENSHAW-CYPHERT | X | | |
| 5. FLANDERS | X | X | X | 18. SIMON-AGAZARIAN (SAVI) | X | X | X |
| 6. FLANDERS (Expanded) | X | | | 19. SMITH (Logic) | X | | |
| 7. GALLAGHER | X | | | 20. SMITH (Strategy) | X | | |
| 8. HONIGMAN (MACI) | X | X | X | 21. SPAULDING (CASES) | X | X | X |
| 9. HOUGH | X | X | | 22. SPAULDING (STARS) | X | X | X |
| 10. HUGHES | X | | | 23. TABA | X | X | |
| 11. JOYCE | X | X | X | 24. WITHALL | X | X | X |
| 12. LINDVALL | X | | | 25. WRIGHT | X | | |
| 13. MEDLEY (OScAR) | X | | | 26. WRIGHT-PROCTOR | X | | |

these measures of what teachers and pupil "do" in the classroom, as contrasted with what they "have" or what they "are" has contributed both to encouraging research results and a feeling of cautious optimism among writers in the field about the potential for building a viable theory of instruction with potential for implementation in practice. This is a major shift from the pessimism expressed prior to the present decade.

## RESEARCH

In general, observation systems have provided a mechanism for describing the role of the teacher as it exists in reality, in contrast with prescriptions found in education liter-

---

*The economist classifies pupil background, teacher background and characteristics as "inputs" into the system. The change in the pupil is the "value added" to supply the desired "outputs." They are the "products" of education. Settings and administrative arrangements (such as team teaching, ungraded, small or large class structures) have often been considered a part of the "process" which generates the "value added." This is not so here. These "arrangements" are considered a part of the input. Only the interaction patterns between the pupil and the teacher (including materials) are considered as the "process."

ature. Descriptive research using observation systems indicates that the role of the teacher appears to be exceedingly consistent across grade levels, subject matter areas and geographic regions. Even under widely divergent circumstances, such as tutoring individual students in an Individually Prescribed Instruction setting, team versus individual teaching, or teaching honors classes contrasted with average or "modified" classes, teacher behaviors do not appear to change in different settings nor with different pupils. The role of the teacher even seems to resist curricular innovations such as new math and physics, a matter of great concern to those who designed the new curriculum to be used in a new way by teachers.

The use of observation instruments provides the educational theorist a way to discern the actual teaching patterns in existing classrooms and then to reformulate models of effective teaching by either 1) learning which teacher behaviors correlate most highly with pupil growth or 2) determining which behaviors teachers are currently using only minimally (or not using at all) which theoretically could contribute to pupil growth.

The bulk of the descriptive studies have related teaching behaviors to pupil outcomes such as attitudes, learning, creativity and change in I.Q. scores. The findings have indicated that those teachers who have more "positive" scores, as measured by the affective systems, seem to have students with better attitudes and higher cognitive achievement. Also those teachers who solicit higher levels of thought as measured by the cognitive systems, tend to have students who produce higher level thought processes. In general, studies indicate that simple memory recall is the most common mental activity solicited by teachers.

Another use of observational systems has been experimental research in which a particular teacher style is theoretically constructed from the categories of a classroom observation system and contrasted with a different teaching style or strategy. In these experiments, a trained role player teaches the same content to two different groups of "matched" students, using two different teaching styles. Both the Flanders and the Miller systems have been used in such experiments and, in general, positive student gains are related to the more indirect and responsive teaching styles. Experiments of this type provide a first step in testing theoretical models of effective teaching.

18

A final step in model development is field testing. This occurs when actual teachers are trained to be able to use a model style or strategy. However, widespread experimental research involving the training of teachers to produce certain types of behavior styles is pretty much an activity of the future. Current activity is primarily limited to model building and to the spelling out of behavioral objectives for certain types of teacher strategies such as inquiry training, raising the thought level of an entire class of pupils, or conducting discussions using an indirect teacher strategy.

Although these models are, in general, not yet ready for field testing, they have provided materials for training teachers, and these strategies are practiced in training programs of those teacher-training institutions possessing the skilled staff resources to implement a program focusing on teacher behavior.

TEACHER TRAINING

Ordinarily when those educators responsible for teacher training modify programs, they change the structure or sequence of these programs. Unfortunately, changes in structure and sequence of professional education courses appear to have little effect on the overt behavior of teachers or student teachers. If teaching behavior is to be changed, then teachers must have an opportunity to study their own teaching and experiment with and practice new teaching behaviors. Only when the focus of the teacher education program is on the teaching act itself can we expect changes or improvement in the behavior of teachers.

Thus, the rationale for using these systems in teacher training is twofold. First, the systems provide a mirror for the teacher to obtain feedback about his own teaching behavior along the dimensions of the particular system used. This feedback provides the teacher with the opportunity to change his own behavior based on data about what he is doing in the classroom. Second, and perhaps more important, many of these systems have been constructed along a theoretical dimension which includes behaviors which are presumed to be helpful in promoting pupil growth if used in the classroom, but which are not ordinarily found in the classrooms of America today. When a teacher uses one of these systems, he gets feedback about the behaviors which he is _not_ using, as well as those which he is. This supplies the chance to learn new behaviors and thus expand the teacher behavior repertoire in ways not ordinarily available to teachers.

Several projects have been run in which teachers were taught to analyze their own behavior. In one type of study, researchers trained teachers to produce specific new behaviors. When teachers used these new behaviors, pupil behaviors changed correspondingly.

Using a different approach, in several studies using the Flanders system, teachers were taught the system itself, were asked to determine for themselves what kinds of behavior they wished to use and were given the opportunity to practice the new behaviors in role-play situations. Given the choice of behaviors to use, they became more indirect, more supportive and less controlling, and their pupils were more highly supported for expanding on their own ideas rather than giving fact-level answers to narrow questions. This implies that teachers do have an interest in becoming more supportive of pupils, but do need to have objective feedback which enables them to know when what they are doing differs from what they want to do. These systems provide a method for checking perception against reality, and this feedback alone may help teachers become more effective without the necessity for an outside monitoring force such as administrative evaluation.

In the past five years, teacher-training institutions increasingly have become aware of the value of providing teachers with a tool with which they can gain objective feedback about their own teaching behaviors. Courses in the use of classroom observation systems are now given in colleges, workshops and in-service training programs and are becoming more easily available both to teacher trainers and to classroom teachers themselves.

## SUPERVISION

Like any other form of evaluation, supervision can be used for two purposes: either to provide feedback for the use of the supervisee, or to supply a rating or grade for the supervisor's use. All too often, supervision is of the latter variety, perhaps because until recently, tools for providing objective feedback about teaching performance have been lacking.

The substitution of classroom observation systems for supervisory rating scales or checksheets fills this lack, for these observation systems separate the descriptive from the evaluative functions of the supervisor. Rating scales are still in far more common use than classroom observation systems even though rating scales have been shown to be more related to the value structure of the person constructing the scale (such as liking or not liking strong disciplinary measures, order in the classroom, good housekeeping practices, rapport with students, etc.) than they are to pupil achievement.

An observer's job is more limited than a rater's, because the observer is forced by the system to describe what is happening. Thus an observer is likely to report such items as the teacher is "asking a question" or "reinforcing a child's search behavior" or "lecturing" or "elaborating on a student statement," but he is not called upon to evaluate these actions while he is observing. To the extent that observation systems are as ideal as possible, personal value judgements by the observer about the actions of the teacher are eliminated, so that the end product tells what actually happened in the classroom, while the end product of a rating schedule more likely tells how the rater felt about what happened in the classroom. The shift from rating scales to observation systems makes it possible for the supervisor to shift his role from boss to partner, that is, from the stereotypic role of evaluator to the more flexible one of professional resource and collaborator. As such, the role of the supervisor becomes one of making available techniques for developing personalized teaching styles in line both with the personality of the teacher and the pupil achievement goals desired.

Obviously, the development of a wider range of teaching styles and the study of their relationship to pupil outcomes has a long way to go. If the goal of supervision is the improvement of teaching rather than the rating of teachers, then the use of objective feedback instruments allows for such supervisory innovations as teachers working together in groups to give each other feedback and to suggest changes. The indications are that teachers who do learn a classroom observation system do change their behaviors in accord with what they want to do, and that school study groups can learn to work together to improve their teaching. (Amidon, Kies, Palisi, 1966)

Educators expect that research findings will make an impact on teaching practice. That is why we do research. Classroom observation instruments are research tools originally designed for collecting research data. In a sense, when teachers use these systems to obtain feedback for self-supervision, they are performing "micro-research" on their own behavior in their own classroom. From this they gain data with which to formulate new hypotheses about the effectiveness of their own teaching technique to test in their next "micro-research" study. It would be strange indeed if it were the methodology of research, rather than the findings, which in the long run changes teaching pratice.

## THE FUTURE

We have talked about the value of the use of these systems to researchers, to teacher trainers, to teachers, and to supervisors. Now what about applications to the be-all and end-all of the education business - the student?

Classrooms are places designed to grow pupils: that is, to help them change. It is a characteristic of our culture that change is usually not based on realistic information but instead is based on fear: "Stop that, or I'll send you to the principal!", "Study hard, or you won't pass the college entrance exams.", etc. Motivation operates only in the present tense, and a great deal of classroom motivation is the creating of enough anxiety about the future to force an action in the present. However, motivation through threat breaks down when the teacher meets a population that appears to have nothing to fear. For example, part of the dread of working with "disadvantaged" children is that they are not afraid of things that they are "supposed" to be afraid of, and therefore the usual arsenal of "motivational" devices does not work. When pupils are not afraid of being scolded, sent out of class, failed or even expelled, what is the poor teacher to do? Clearly, a new approach is needed.

Classrooms are places designed to help pupils continue to grow: that is, to provide the skills to allow students to learn, even when they are not in school. But in most schools the curriculum is geared to memorizing facts. "List the 92 elements" - (or is it 98, or 101, or 121?). In a world where half of the products we consume didn't exist when we were born, memory alone has limited utility and "education for life" can no longer mean, "I've learned all I need to know." In our culture, rote is no longer right, if it ever was. The rapid changes in our culture are leaving our schools behind and largely out of touch with the reality of here and now, to say nothing of leaving them without the means of preparing pupils for the reality of a tomorrow we can scarcely imagine.

We believe that observation instruments offer a way to change education. These tools have a promising future as subject matter content. Children themselves can be taught these systems so that they can monitor both their own approaches to learning and their own patterns of behavior.

For instance, most pupils do not want to hear things that are unpleasant about themselves, but receiving and using data about themselves (both positive and negative) is how pupils grow. Acquiring and processing data about oneself is a way of confronting reality, and teaching pupils descriptive systems by which they can get (and give) descriptive and non-evaluative "feedback" from peers and teachers alike seems to be one way of taking a giant step forward in bringing the classroom closer to the reality that both pupils and teachers experience outside the classroom.

Techniques can be developed for students to practice and evaluate their reactions to, and awareness of, their own feelings and the feelings of others. Children learn to differentiate between varying types of verbal behavior very early. Proposals or descriptions are very different from self-defensive and hostile statements. Having pupils practice varying verbal patterns and helping them identify the effects of these patterns on others should improve pupils' ability to communicate.

A pupil can learn about individual differences by noting that people have different tolerances for the amount and kinds of data they are comfortable sharing, and he can learn to hear other people's opinions of him as their opinions and not necessarily as facts about him. He can learn to separate opinion from data, learn to "own" his own feelings so that he doesn't talk about "we" or "they" when he means "I," and can learn to "check out" his perceptions of reality by collecting feedback data.

The possession of these skills lessens both the generation-gap problems and the cultural-gap problems so often present between the faculty and students in our urban schools. Even more important to the learning process is the likelihood that teaching children the skills of affective discrimination is a direct way to develop a sense of self-worth, self-motivation and self-direction.

In the cognitive area, recall, data processing, and evaluation are very different from each other. When verbalized, these differences become apparent and clearly separable. When they are, they can be identified and new judgements can be made about their appropriateness to any given situation. It appears then that verbal interaction systems can be modified for use as content in such a way that pupils can acquire the ability to "evaluate" their own data processing techniques. Further, they can learn to develop criteria for choosing appropriate cognitive sequences to match against problem types, and can literally learn to improve their own probability of success. Such adaptations are a major concern of the editors and their colleagues.

A good education is hard to come by but its description is easy to state: An educated person is one who can recognize a problem as a problem the first time he sees it and has optimized his chances for solving it. How to solve problems; how to communicate; and how to know, "be," and accept oneself are only now becoming a direct concern of curriculum builders. In our culture these skills are prerequisite to effective, productive living. And helping students acquire the tools for self-evaluation and improvement of perceptual, communication and problem-solving skills is a job that schools must do. These "behavior mirrors" supply the first objective tools for teaching and evaluating both cognitive and affective skills that education has had.

24

# ANTHOLOGY OF CLASSROOM OBSERVATION INSTRUMENTS

Abstracted from

# INTERACTION ANALYSIS: RECENT DEVELOPMENTS*

Edmund J. Amidon

* Paper delivered at the American Education Research Association Annual Convention, Chicago, Illinois,
February, 1966.

# MODIFIED CATEGORY SYSTEM (MCS) SUMMARY

**1**

| * | ** | SYSTEM DIMENSION |
|---|----|------------------|
| X | 19 | Affective |
| X | 16 | Cognitive |
|   | 6  | Work process (control) |
|   | 4  | Behavior |

### TYPE OF COMMUNICATION RECORDED

| * | ** | |
|---|----|--|
| X | 25 | Verbal |
|   | 7  | Nonverbal |

### SUBJECT OF OBSERVATION

| * | ** | |
|---|----|--|
|   | 5  | Teacher only |
|   | 2  | Student only |
| X | 19 | Teacher and student |

### DATA COLLECTION METHODS REPORTED

| * | ** | |
|---|----|--|
| X | 18 | Live |
| X | 13 | Tape recording without tapescript |
|   | 9  | Tape recording and tapescript |
|   | 13 | Video tape |
|   | 1  | Handwritten notes |

### AUDIO OR VIDEO TAPE REQUIRED

| * | ** | |
|---|----|--|
|   | 9  | Yes |
| X | 17 | No |

### PERSONNEL NEEDED FOR OBSERVATION OR RECORDING SESSION

| * | ** | |
|---|----|--|
| X | 17 | 1 coder |
|   | 1  | Team of 2 |
|   | 1  | 2 teams of 2 |
|   | 9  | Tape operator |

### NUMBER OF CODERS NEEDED DURING CODING SESSION

| * | ** | |
|---|----|--|
| X | 17 | No coder other than observer(s) |
|   | 3  | 1 coder |
|   | 2  | 2 coders |
|   | 4  | 2 teams of 2 coders |

### CODING UNITS

| * | ** | |
|---|----|--|
|   | 18 | Category change |
| X | 9  | Category + time unit |
|   | 6  | Content area change |
|   | 3  | Speaker change |
|   | 3  | Time sample |

### USES REPORTED BY AUTHOR

| * | ** | |
|---|----|--|
| X | 26 | Research |
|   | 12 | Teacher training |
|   | 9  | Supervision |

* Summary of information for this system

** Summary of information for 26 systems

# MODIFIED CATEGORY SYSTEM

This system was created when a seminar was formed by staff of the College of Education at Temple University interested in the improvement of teaching. Each member assumed responsibility for thoroughly learning about one or two classroom observation systems, and then taught the material to the others in the seminar. The systems reviewed, aside from that of Flanders with which the group was already thoroughly familiar, were Aschner-Gallagher, Medley (OScAR 4V), Hughes-Miller, Simon and Agazarian (SAVI), Smith (Strategies), Smith (Logic) and Taba.

The resulting Modified Category System was an integration of the cognitive categories from other systems into the framework of the Flanders systems, thus creating a new system containing both affective and cognitive dimensions. The ten categories of the Flanders system form the core of the new system and categories from other systems are nested into the Flanders categories. For example: category 2 (praise in the Flanders System) and category 7 (criticism in the Flanders System) have been expanded to include categories from the Hughes-Miller System as follows:

2a (7a) - Praises (Criticizes) using Public criteria

2b (7b) - Praises (Criticizes) using Private criteria

Another example, category 4 (questions in the Flanders system), has been expanded to include four generalized categories from the Aschner-Gallagher system:

4. Asks:  a - Cognitive Memory Question

b - Convergent Question

c - Divergent Question

d - Evaluative Question

Student talk categories 8 and 9 in the Flanders system have been expanded by including from the Taba system the thought process indicated by students talking on a descriptive, inferential, or generalization level.

This is an attempt to build a category system simple enough to be used "live" by an observer in a classroom, but incorporating affective and cognitive dimensions from other systems into the Flanders base.

## OBSERVER RELIABILITY PROCEDURES

Scott coefficient is used to calculate reliability. Range of reliability reported is .87 to .92.

## SUPPLEMENTARY MATERIAL

Amidon, Edmund J., "Interaction Analysis: Recent Developments." Paper presented at the American Educational Research Association Convention, Chicago, February, 1966.

# CATEGORIES FOR
## MODIFIED CATEGORY SYSTEM

### Edmund J. Amidon

---

**TEACHER TALK**

1. Accepts Feeling

2a. Praises
2b. Praises Using Public Criteria
2c. Praises Using Private Criteria

3. Accepts Idea Through: a) Description
                              b) Inference
                              c) Generalization

4. Asks: a) Cognitive Memory Question
           b) Convergent Question
           c) Divergent Question
           d) Evaluative Question

5. Lectures

6. Gives Direction

7a. Criticizes
7b. Criticizes Using Public Criteria
7c. Criticizes Using Private Criteria

---

**STUDENT TALK**

8. Pupil Response: a) Description
                     b) Inference
                     c) Generalization

9. Pupil Initiation: a) Description
                     b) Inference
                     c) Generalization

---

10. Silence

11. Confusion

Abstracted from

# VERBAL INTERACTION CATEGORY SYSTEM (VICS)*

Edmund J. Amidon
Elizabeth Hunter

*From **Improving Teaching: Analyzing Verbal Interaction in the Classroom.** New York: Holt, Rinehart & Winston, Inc., 1966, pp. 209-221.

# VERBAL INTERACTION CATEGORY SYSTEM (VICS) SUMMARY

### SYSTEM DIMENSION

| * | ** | |
|---|----|---|
| X | 19 | Affective |
|   | 16 | Cognitive |
|   | 6  | Work process (control) |
|   | 4  | Behavior |

### TYPE OF COMMUNICATION RECORDED

| X | 25 | Verbal |
|---|----|--------|
|   | 7  | Nonverbal |

### SUBJECT OF OBSERVATION

|   | 5  | Teacher only |
|---|----|--------------|
|   | 2  | Student only |
| X | 19 | Teacher and student |

### DATA COLLECTION METHODS REPORTED

| X | 18 | Live |
|---|----|------|
| X | 13 | Tape recording without tapescript |
|   | 9  | Tape recording and tapescript |
|   | 13 | Video tape |
|   | 1  | Handwritten notes |

### AUDIO OR VIDEO TAPE REQUIRED

|   | 9  | Yes |
|---|----|-----|
| X | 17 | No |

### PERSONNEL NEEDED FOR OBSERVATION OR RECORDING SESSION

| X | 17 | 1 coder |
|---|----|---------|
|   | 1  | Team of 2 |
|   | 1  | 2 teams of 2 |
|   | 9  | Tape operator |

### NUMBER OF CODERS NEEDED DURING CODING SESSION

| X | 17 | No coder other than observer(s) |
|---|----|---------------------------------|
|   | 3  | 1 coder |
|   | 2  | 2 coders |
|   | 4  | 2 teams of 2 coders |

### CODING UNITS

|   | 18 | Category change |
|---|----|-----------------|
| X | 9  | Category + time unit |
|   | 6  | Content area change |
|   | 3  | Speaker change |
|   | 3  | Time sample |

### USES REPORTED BY AUTHOR

| X | 26 | Research |
|---|----|----------|
| X | 12 | Teacher training |
| X | 9  | Supervision |

* Summary of information for this system

** Summary of information for 26 systems

# VICS - VERBAL INTERACTION CATEGORY SYSTEM

This system expands the Flanders System in order to provide more detailed information. It has provisions for recording not only those times when the teacher accepts or rejects the ideas and feelings of the pupil, but also when he accepts or rejects the pupil's nonverbal behavior.

The separation of acceptance and rejection into three dimensions (ideas, feelings and behaviors) allows for analysis of such subtle differences in teacher style as that of a teacher skillful enough to accept a child's feelings at the same time as criticizing his ideas thus correcting him on the cognitive level on the one hand and accepting him on the emotional or affective level on the other.

In addition the categories which reveal how a teacher responds to pupils' behaviors provide some measure of the physical freedom allowed the pupils.

VICS, like the Flanders System, also has provision for noting whether the student is responding to talk from the teacher or initiating statements to the teacher and unlike the Flanders system, has provision for noting whether the student is responding or initiating talk to another pupil. It also separates the "silence" from the "confusion" category.

## OBSERVER RELIABILITY PROCEDURES

No range of reliability scores were reported by the authors.

## SUPPLEMENTARY MATERIALS

Amidon, Edmund J. and Hunter, Elizabeth. Improving Teaching: Analyzing Verbal Interaction in the Classroom. New York: Holt, Rinehart, and Winston, Inc., 1966, pp. 209-221.

CATEGORIES FOR

## THE VERBAL INTERACTION CATEGORY SYSTEM (VICS)

Edmund J. Amidon and Elizabeth Hunter

---

| | | |
|---|---|---|
| Teacher - Initiated Talk | 1. | Gives Information or Opinion: presents content or own ideas, explains, orients, asks rhetorical questions. May be short statements or extended lecture. |
| | 2. | Gives Direction: tells pupil to take some specific action; gives orders; commands. |
| | 3. | Asks Narrow Question: asks drill questions, questions requiring one or two word replies or yes-or-no answers; questions to which the specific nature of the response can be predicted. |
| | 4. | Asks Broad Question: asks relatively open-ended questions which call for unpredictable response; questions which are thought-provoking. Apt to elicit a longer response than 3. |

---

| | | |
|---|---|---|
| Teacher's Response | 5. | Accepts: |
| | | (5a) Ideas: reflects, clarifies, encourages or praises ideas of pupils. Summarizes, or comments without rejection. |
| | | (5b) Behavior: responds in ways which commend, encourage or acknowledge pupil behavior. |
| | | (5c) Feeling: responds in ways which reflect or encourage expression of pupil feeling. |
| | 6. | Rejects: |
| | | (6a) Ideas: criticizes, ignores or discourages pupil ideas. |
| | | (6b) Behavior: discourages or criticizes pupil behavior. Designed to stop undesirable behavior. May be stated in question form, but differentiated from category 3 or 4, and from category 2, Gives Direction, by tone of voice and resultant effect on pupils. |
| | | (6c) Feeling: ignores, discourages, or rejects pupil expression of feeling. |

---

| | | | |
|---|---|---|---|
| Pupil Response | 7. | Responds to Teacher: | (7a) Predictably: relatively short replies, usually, which follow category 3. May also follow category 2, i.e. "David, you may read next." |
| | | | (7b) Unpredictably: replies which usually follow category 4. |
| | 8. | Responds to Another Pupil: replies occurring in conversation between pupils. | |
| Pupil-Initiated Talk | 9. | Initiates Talk to Teacher: statements which pupils direct to teacher without solicitation from teacher. | |
| | 10. | Initiates Talk to Another Pupil: statements which pupils direct to another pupil which are not solicited. | |
| Other | 11. | Silence: pauses or short periods of silence during a time of classroom conversation. | |
| | Z. | Confusion: considerable noise which disrupts planned activities. This category may accompany other categories or may totally preclude the use of other categories. | |

3

Abstracted from

# ASCHNER-GALLAGHER SYSTEM FOR CLASSIFYING THOUGHT PROCESSES IN THE CONTEXT OF CLASSROOM VERBAL INTERACTION*

Mary Jane Aschner    James J. Gallagher

Joyce M. Perry    Sibel S. Afsar

William Jenne    Helen Farr

*Published by Institute for Research on Exceptional Children, University of Illinois, 1965.
The development of this System was made possible by a grant from the Cooperative Research Program (Project #965—Productive Thinking of Gifted Children) and from the Elizabeth McCormick Memorial Fund, Chicago, Illinois.

each. Each team arrives at a consensus of judgements and then those team judgements are compared. Range of reliability reported by the author is 75 to 80% agreement.

## SUPPLEMENTARY MATERIAL

Aschner, Mary Jane and Gallagher, James J., et al. A System for Classifying Thought Processes in the Context of Classroom Verbal Interaction. Chicago: University of Illinois, Institute for Research on Exceptional Children, 1965.

# CATEGORIES FOR
## ASCHNER-GALLAGHER SYSTEM

### Mary Jane Aschner and James J. Gallagher

## I. ROUTINE (R)

This category includes routine classroom procedural matters such as management of the classroom, the structuring of class discussion and approval or disapproval of the idea or the person.

MANAGEMENT ............................................................

Mq - <u>Question:</u> Requests or invitations to speak; calling for questions, as in "Anybody have a question?" ............................................

Mp - <u>Procedure:</u> Announcements or procedural instructions, given or requested for individuals or the group as a whole ...............................

Ma - <u>Aside:</u> Incidental or parenthetical comment; gratuitous content............

Mnc - <u>Nose-Counting:</u> Calling for or responding with a show of hands for a tally or canvas .......................................................

Mfb - <u>Feedback:</u> Request for or response with signs from group as to whether or not the speaker's actions or remarks are clearly understood ..............

Mw - <u>Work:</u> Non-verbal actions or seatwork going on in connection with current discussion or class proceedings ......................................

X - Unclassifiable response primarily due to technical recording difficulties ....

STRUCTURING ...........................................................

Sts - <u>Self-Structuring:</u> Conventional prefatory move to signal content and purport of one's own next remarks or behavior.......................

Sto - <u>Structuring Other (s):</u> Engineering next speech or actions of other (s). Monitoring other's performance. Pump-priming to keep discussion going on a point already before the class ..............................

Stf - <u>Future Structuring:</u> Forecast of future activity, study, learning, etc. beyond this particular class session................................

Stc - <u>Class Structuring:</u> Focusing class attention on point to be emphasized or taken up; laying groundwork for question or problem; probing, pushing, adding data for bogged-down class (teacher only).................

VERDICT ...............................................................

Ver - <u>Verdict</u>: (+ or -) Impersonal praise or reproach on quality of academic performance of individual or group ............................

Verp - <u>Personal Verdict</u>: (+ or -) Personal praise or reproach of individual. (Occasionally by T on whole class) Negative Verp generally on deportment .

Agr - <u>Agreement</u>: (+ or -) Acceptance or rejection of content: conceding a point; not permission-giving nor procedural ............................

S - <u>Self Reference</u>: Speaker's personal report or comment upon or about self. Often conventional device; cautionary tactic .....................

Du - <u>Dunno</u>: Explicit indication that one does not know ..................

Mu - <u>Muddled</u>: Speaker confused, mixed up, flustered ....................

Hu - <u>Humor</u>: Remark of evident witty, humorous, or comic intent; response (usually laughter) to same ...............................

## II. COGNITIVE-MEMORY (C-M)

C-M operations represent the simple reproduction of facts, formulas and other items of remembered content through use of such processes as recognition, rote memory and selective recall.

Scr - <u>Scribe</u>: Giving a spoken or written spelling or exemplification of a word or expression .....................................

RECAPITULATION .........................................................

Req - <u>Quoting:</u> Rote recitation or literal reading from text, paper or notes in hand ...................................................

Rep - <u>Repetition</u>: Literal or nearly verbatim restatement of something just said . .

Rec - <u>Recounting:</u> Narration of past extra-class occurrence ...................

Rev - <u>Review</u>: Recitation of material which occurred or was discussed in current or past class session ......................................

CLARIFICATION ..........................................................

Clm - <u>Clarifying Meaning</u>: Rendering a previous statement more intelligible either by (a) restating or rephrasing or (b) adding informative details ...........

Clq - <u>Clarifying Qualification</u>: Render a previous statement more accurate either by (a) "Entering a rider" upon the remark or (b) entering an explicit correction ..............................................

FACTUAL .................................................................

      Fs  -  <u>Fact Stating:</u>  Requests for and recitations of items taken to be matters of fact .................................................

      Fd  -  <u>Fact Detailing:</u> Spinning out further a prior assertion of fact or other statements (As, Exr) in which factual items were mentioned. .............

      Fm  -  <u>Factual Monologue:</u> Reporting of factual material in the form of a monologue during which verbal exchange is conventionally excluded .................

## III.  CONVERGENT THINKING

Convergent thinking is thought operation involving the analysis and integration of given or remembered data.  It leads to one expected result because of the tightly structured framework which limits it.

TRANSLATION  .........................................................

      Tr  -  <u>Translation:</u> Shift of conceptual material from symbolic or figural content to semantic, or vice versa .........................................

ASSOCIATION .........................................................

      As  -  <u>Association:</u> Involving likenesses and differences; degrees of comparison; and relationship of direction, spatial position and/or classification, etc ....

EXPLANATION ........................................................

      Exr  -  <u>Rational Explanation:</u> Asking or telling why X is the case; why Y caused X, etc.  Substantiating a claim or conclusion by citing evidence..............

      Exv  -  <u>Value Explanation:</u> Asking or telling why X is good, bad, useful, important, etc.  Justifying a rating, viewpoint, or value-based judgment by giving reasons why..............................................

      Exn  -  <u>Narrative Explanation:</u> Step-by-step account of how something is done, how a mechanism works, or of what led up to an event or given outcome ........

CONCLUSION ........................................................

      Gen  -  <u>Generalization:</u>  Integration of prior remarks by slightly more general reformulation ..................................................

      Cons  -  <u>Summary Conclusion:</u>  Summary reformulation, often serial or enumerative, of material treated in discussion or reading ............................

      Conl  -  <u>Logical Conclusion:</u>  Calling for a deductively drawn implication from material presented ...............................................

# EVALUATIVE THINKING (ET)

Evaluative thinking deals with matters of value rather than matters of fact and is characterized by verbal performance by its judgemental character.

UNSTRUCTURED ..................................................................

Ura  -  Unstructured Rating:  A value judgment produced or requested on some idea or item in terms of a scale of values provided by the respondent ...........

Uju  -  Unstructured Judgment:  A value judgment produced or requested on some idea or item wherein the value dimension has already been provided ......

STRUCTURED ....................................................................

Svp  -  Structured Probability:  An estimate or speculative opinion is given or requested as to the likelihood of some occurrence or situation .............

Svc  -  Structured Choice:  Speaker calls for or declares his position as a choice between alternatives (not between Yes or No answers) ...................

QUALIFICATION .................................................................

Qj  -  Qualified Judgment:  An offer or request for a rider or modification to a prior value judgment.  Also, attempts to make more precise the value dimension discussed ..........................................................

Qc  -  Counter Judgment:  Speaker declares a directly opposed position with respect to value statement of a previous classroom speaker ..............

## V.  DIVERGENT THINKING (DT)

In a Divergent Thinking sequence, individuals are free to independently generate their own data within a data-poor situation, often taking a new direction or perspective.

El  -  Elaboration:  Structured or free (s or f)  Building upon a point already made; filling out or developing a point, but not shifting to a new point, often by concocting instances or examples ....................................

Ad  -  Divergent Association:  (s or f) Constructing a relationship between ideas, casting the central idea into sharper and often unexpected perspective, by comparisons, analogies, etc. .............................................

Imp  -  Implication:  (s or f) Extrapolation beyond the given, projection from given data--typically by antecedent -- consequent or hypothetical construction -- to new point (s) of possibility ........................................

Syn  -  Synthesis:  Spontaneous performance, tying in, integrating the current central idea with an entirely new point or frame of reference.  May be a variation or reversal of a previous conclusion .................................

Double-paired Ratings:  The complex nature of verbal classroom interaction often requires the combination of more than one of the above described categories.

4

Abstracted from

# THE LANGUAGE OF THE CLASSROOM*

Arno A. Bellack
Herbert M. Kliebard
Ronald T. Hyman
Frank L. Smith, Jr.

*Published by Teachers College Press, Teachers College, Columbia University, New York, 1966.

# BELLACK SYSTEM SUMMARY

**4**

### SYSTEM DIMENSION

| * | ** | |
|---|---|---|
|  | 19 | Affective |
| X | 16 | Cognitive |
|  | 6 | Work process (control) |
|  | 4 | Behavior |

### TYPE OF COMMUNICATION RECORDED

| * | ** | |
|---|---|---|
| X | 25 | Verbal |
|  | 7 | Nonverbal |

### SUBJECT OF OBSERVATION

| * | ** | |
|---|---|---|
|  | 5 | Teacher only |
|  | 2 | Student only |
| X | 19 | Teacher and student |

### DATA COLLECTION METHODS REPORTED

| * | ** | |
|---|---|---|
|  | 18 | Live |
|  | 13 | Tape recording without tapescript |
| X | 9 | Tape recording and tapescript |
|  | 13 | Video tape |
|  | 1 | Handwritten notes |

### AUDIO OR VIDEO TAPE REQUIRED

| * | ** | |
|---|---|---|
| X | 9 | Yes |
|  | 17 | No |

### PERSONNEL NEEDED FOR OBSERVATION OR RECORDING SESSION

| * | ** | |
|---|---|---|
|  | 17 | 1 coder |
|  | 1 | Team of 2 |
|  | 1 | 2 teams of 2 |
| X | 9 | Tape operator |

### NUMBER OF CODERS NEEDED DURING CODING SESSION

| * | ** | |
|---|---|---|
|  | 17 | No coder other than observer(s) |
|  | 3 | 1 coder |
|  | 2 | 2 coders |
| X | 4 | 2 teams of 2 coders |

### CODING UNITS

| * | ** | |
|---|---|---|
| X | 18 | Category change |
|  | 9 | Category + time unit |
|  | 6 | Content area change |
| X | 3 | Speaker change |
|  | 3 | Time sample |

### USES REPORTED BY AUTHOR

| * | ** | |
|---|---|---|
| X | 26 | Research |
|  | 12 | Teacher training |
|  | 9 | Supervision |

* Summary of information for this system

** Summary of information for 26 systems

# THE BELLACK SYSTEM

This complex system requires that classroom interaction be tape recorded for later analysis by coders. Several sets of information are coded about each statement:

1) The speaker is coded, whether teacher or pupil.

2) The type of pedagogical move is coded in one of four categories so that the coder records whether the speaker is 1) structuring, 2) soliciting, 3) responding to a solicitation (giving an answer, for example), or 4) reacting to a response (clarifying, evaluating or modifying).

3) The "substantive" meaning is coded (somewhat like a content analysis, that is, the coder records what the teacher and pupil are talking about).

4) The "substantive-logical" meaning is given. These categories are very similar to those of the Smith System, "The Logic of Teaching." In this area the coder codes whether the teacher or student is doing such things as defining, fact stating, explaining, justifying, etc.

5) The sum of the number of lines on the tapescript in 3 and 4 above, are coded to determine how much the teachers and how much the pupils talk about the content.

6) The function of the dialogue with respect to factors of classroom management is coded in "instructional meanings" for such matters as the teacher is giving homework assignments or having the students go up to the blackboard.

7) The kind of logical process the teacher has used to handle this instructional management is coded.

and

8) The number of tapescript lines of activity when the teacher is handling classroom management is counted so that the amount of teacher and student talk in this area can be determined.

Bellack used this system to collect data about high school teaching, and found that cycles of teacher and pupil behaviors are rather consistent from classroom to classroom; almost as if teachers and pupils were playing a game with well defined rules.

Bellack spells out the "rules of the classroom game" in some detail citing rules for the pupil, such as, the pupil does not set forth regulations, and the pupil structures less than he solicits, responds or reacts. This indicates pupils do not take initiative in the classroom. Rules for the teacher require that the teacher will structure the lesson, and will do most of the questioning and most of the reacting to pupil answers. In addition, the teacher will be the most active person in the classroom and will talk more than the pupils. Bellack also studies cycles of teacher-pupil interaction. The two basic cycles of "Solicitation followed by Response," and "Solicitation followed by Response followed by Reaction" account for more than 48 percent of all teaching cycles. In addition, the question-answer cycle comprises the core of most other teaching cycles, therefore teachers in general do not seem to deviate radically from a general teaching pattern that consists basically of asking questions and receiving answers. (Solicitation followed by Response pattern.)

Bellack's teaching cycles can be used to stimulate teachers to consider the effects of breaking the rules of the classroom game, and creating classroom climates in which, for instance, the teacher is not the most active member of the class, or in which the pupils do evaluate the teacher and evaluate each other, or in which the pupils do the questioning and reacting.

Although the system was designed for use in economics classes, it can be adapted for use in any subject matter area.

## OBSERVER RELIABILITY PROCEDURES

Four coders divide into two teams. One member of each team codes a given sample. The other member reviews the coding. Both members of each team arbitrate disagreements between coder and reviewer. The percentage of agreement is computed in terms of number of lines and number of moves.

The range of reliability reported by the author is .84 to .96.

## SUPPLEMENTARY MATERIALS

Computer Programs prepared for IBM 7090 computer. (Computes numbers and percentages of lines of transcripts in each category and moves in each category.)

Bellack, Arno, Kliebard, Herbert, Hyman, Ronald and Smith, Frank. The Language of the Classroom. (Includes Part I and II of The Language of the Classroom, Meanings Communicated in High School Teaching.) Teachers College Press. Columbia University, 1966.

CATEGORIES FOR
THE BELLACK SYSTEM

Arno A. Bellack
Herbert M. Kliebard
Ronald T. Hyman
Frank L. Smith, Jr.

## SUMMARY OF THE CODING SYSTEM[1]

(1) SPEAKER: indicates source of utterance

Teacher (T); Pupil (P); Audio-Visual Device (A)

(2) TYPE OF PEDAGOGICAL MOVE: reference to function of move

Initiatory Moves
Structuring (STR): sets context for subsequent behavior by launching or halting-excluding interaction
Soliciting (SOL): directly elicits verbal, physical, or mental response; coded in terms of response expected
Reflexive Moves
Responding (RES): fulfills expectation of solicitation; bears reciprocal relation only to solicitation
Reacting (REA): modifies (by clarifying, synthesizing, expanding) and/or rates (positively or negatively): occasioned by previous move, but not directly elicited; reactions to more than one previous move coded REA
Not Codable (NOC): function uncertain because tape is inaudible

(3) SUBSTANTIVE MEANING: reference to subject matter topic. (Based on a content analysis of the pamphlet by Calderwood)

Trade (TRA)
    Trade -- Domestic and International (TDI)
    Trade -- Money and Banking (TMB)
    Trade -- Who Trades with Whom (TWH)
Factors of Production and/or Specialization (FSP)
    Factor of Production -- Natural Resources (FNR)
    Factor of Production -- Human Skills (FHS)
    Factor of Production -- Capital Equipment (FCE)
    Factors Other Than Natural Resources, Human Skills, and Capital Equipment Occurring in Discussion of Reasons for Trade (FRE)
Imports and/or Exports (IMX)
Foreign Investment -- General (FOR)
    Foreign Investment -- Direct (FOD)
    Foreign Investment -- Portfolio (FOP)

---

[1]Underlining indicates actual coding terminology.

Barriers to Trade (BAR)
    Barrier -- Tariffs (BAT)
    Barrier -- Quotas (BAQ)
    Barrier -- Exchange Control (BAE)
    Barrier -- Export Control (BAX)
    Barrier -- Administrative Protectionism (BAA)
Promoting Free Trade (PFT)
Relevant to Trade (REL)
Not Trade (NTR)

(4) SUBSTANTIVE - LOGICAL MEANING: reference to cognitive process involved in dealing with the subject matter under study

Analytic Process:  Proposed use of language or established rules of logic
  Defining-General (DEF): defining characteristics of class or term with example of items within class explicitly given
    Defining-Denotative (DED): object referent of term
    Defining-Connotative (DEC): detinining characteristics of class or term
    Interpreting (INT): verbal equivalent of a statement, slogan, aphorism, or proverb
Empirical Process: sense experience as criterion of truth
  Fact Stating (FAC): what is, was, or will be without explanation or evaluation; account, report, description, statement of event or state of affairs
  Explaining (XPL): relation between objects, events, principles; conditional inference; cause-effect; explicit comparison contrast; statement of principles, theories or laws

Evaluative Process: set of criteria or value system as basis for verification
  Opining (OPN): personal values for statement of policy, judgment or evaluation of event, idea, state of affairs; direct and indirect evaluation included
  Justifying (JUS): reasons or argument for or against opinion or judgment

Logical Process Not Clear (NCL): cognitive process involved not clear

(5) NUMBER OF LINES IN 3 AND 4 ABOVE

(6) INSTRUCTIONAL MEANINGS: reference to factors related to classroom management

Assignment (ASG) suggested or required student activity; reports, tests, readings, debates, homework, etc.
Material (MAT): teaching aids and instructional devices
Person (PER): person as physical object or personal experiences
Procedure (PRC): a plan of activities or a course of action
Statement (STA): verbal utterance, particularly the meaning, validity, truth or propriety of an utterance
Logical Process (LOG): function of language or rule of logic; reference to definitions or arguments, but not presentation of such
Action-General (ACT): performance (vocal, non-vocal, cognitive, or emotional) the specific nature of which is uncertain or complex
Action-Vocal (ACV): physical qualities of vocal action
Action-Physical (ACP): physical movement or process
Action-Cognitive (ACC): cognitive process, but not the language or logic of a specific utterance; thinking, knowing, understanding, listening
Action-Emotional (ACE): emotion or feeling, but not expression of attitude or value
Language Mechanics (LAM): the rules of grammar and/or usage

(7) INSTRUCTIONAL-LOGICAL MEANING: reference to cognitive processes related to the distinctly didactic verbal moves in the instructional situation

    Analytic Process: see (4) above
       Defining-General (DEF)
          Defining-Denotative (DED)
          Defining-Connotative (DEC)
       Interpreting (INT)
    Empirical Process: see (4) above
       Fact Stating (FAC)
       Explaining (XPL)
    Evaluative Process
       Opining (OPN): see (4) above
       Justifying (JUS): see (4) above
       Rating: reference to metacommunication; usually an evaluative reaction (REA)
          Positive(POS): distinctly affirmative evaluation
          Admitting (ADM): mild or equivocally positive evaluation
          Repeating (RPT): implicit positive evaluation when statement (STA) is repeated by another speaker; also for SOL to repeat vocal action (ACV)
          Qualifying (QAL): explicit reservation stated in evaluation; exception
          Not Admitting (NAD): evaluation which rejects by stating the contrary; direct refutation or correction excluded
          Negative (NEG): distinctly negative evaluation
          Positive/Negative (PON): SOL requesting positive or negative evaluation
          Admitting/Not Admitting (AON): SOL asking to permit or not permit procedure or action
    Extralogical Process: SOL expecting physical action or when logical nature of verbal response cannot be determined
       Performing (PRF): asking, demanding, explicit directive or imperative
       Directing (DIR); SOL with or without stated alternatives; asking for directive, not permission for specific action

(8) NUMBER OF LINES IN 6 and 7 ABOVE

Each pedagogical move is coded as follows:

   (1) / (2) / (3) / (4) / (5) / (6) / (7) / (8)

    (1) Speaker
    (2) Type of Pedagogical Move
    (3) Substantive Meaning
    (4) Substantive-Logical Meaning
    (5) Number of Typescript Lines in (3) and (4)
    (6) Instructional Meaning
    (7) Instructional-Logical Meaning
    (8) Number of Typescript Lines in (6) and (7)

# CODING THE PROTOCOLS

The following excerpt from one of the coded protocols illustrates the coding procedures and interpretations of the coded information.

Excerpt From Protocol

Teacher (Move #1): Now, in order to pacify, or help satisfy, certain groups in American industry and American politics who want high protective tariffs, or who are clamoring for protection, we have inserted into our reciprocal agreements two --what you might call -- safeguards which are coming up now as President Kennedy looks for greater authority in the tariff business. (Move #2) What have we inserted in here to give an element of protection or to stifle the outcries of American businessmen who want protection? Two clauses which we call . . . ? Yes?
Pupil (Move #3): The peril point and the escape clause.
Teacher (Move #4): Right. The peril point and the escape clause.

Code

```
Move #1 T/STR / BAT / XPL / 8 / - / - / -
Move #2 T/SOL / BAT / FAC / 4 / - / - / -
Move #3 P/RES / BAT / FAC / 1 / - / - / -
Move #4 T/REA / BAT /  - /  - / STA / POS/ 1
```

Interpretation

The teacher focuses on a substantive area by explaining something having to do with tariffs to the extent of seven lines (Move #1). He then solicits for three lines with the expectation that a factual response on tariffs will be given (Move #2). A pupil gives a one-line response by stating a fact about tariffs (Move #3). The teacher positively evaluates the statement by the pupil (Move #4).

The entire segment of discourse is an example of a teacher-initiated cycle 9 (STR SOL RES REA).

5

Abstracted from

# INTERACTION ANALYSIS IN THE CLASSROOM
# A MANUAL FOR OBSERVERS*

**Ned A. Flanders**

*Published by University of Michigan, School of Education, Ann Arbor, Michigan, Revised Edition, 1966.

# FLANDERS SYSTEM OF INTERACTION ANALYSIS (FSIA) SUMMARY

**5**

|  | * | ** | SYSTEM DIMENSION |
|---|---|---|---|
|  | X | 19 | Affective |
|  |  | 16 | Cognitive |
|  |  | 6 | Work process (control) |
|  |  | 4 | Behavior |

### TYPE OF COMMUNICATION RECORDED

| * | ** |  |
|---|---|---|
| X | 25 | Verbal |
|  | 7 | Nonverbal |

### SUBJECT OF OBSERVATION

| * | ** |  |
|---|---|---|
|  | 5 | Teacher only |
|  | 2 | Student only |
| X | 19 | Teacher and student |

### DATA COLLECTION METHODS REPORTED

| * | ** |  |
|---|---|---|
| X | 18 | Live |
| X | 13 | Tape recording without tapescript |
|  | 9 | Tape recording and tapescript |
| X | 13 | Video tape |
|  | 1 | Handwritten notes |

### AUDIO OR VIDEO TAPE REQUIRED

| * | ** |  |
|---|---|---|
|  | 9 | Yes |
| X | 17 | No |

### PERSONNEL NEEDED FOR OBSERVATION OR RECORDING SESSION

| * | ** |  |
|---|---|---|
| X | 17 | 1 coder |
|  | 1 | Team of 2 |
|  | 1 | 2 teams of 2 |
|  | 9 | Tape operator |

### NUMBER OF CODERS NEEDED DURING CODING SESSION

| * | ** |  |
|---|---|---|
| X | 17 | No coder other than observer(s) |
|  | 3 | 1 coder |
|  | 2 | 2 coders |
|  | 4 | 2 teams of 2 coders |

### CODING UNITS

| * | ** |  |
|---|---|---|
|  | 18 | Category change |
| X | 9 | Category + time unit |
|  | 6 | Content area change |
|  | 3 | Speaker change |
|  | 3 | Time sample |

### USES REPORTED BY AUTHOR

| * | ** |  |
|---|---|---|
| X | 26 | Research |
| X | 12 | Teacher training |
| X | 9 | Supervision |

\* Summary of information for this system

\*\* Summary of information for 26 systems

# THE FLANDERS SYSTEM OF
# INTERACTION ANALYSIS

The Flanders System of Interaction Analysis, the most widely used classroom observation system, contains only ten categories. This system can be used "live" by an observer coding while sitting in the classroom, and does not require tape recording the interaction for playback purposes for later coding.

Despite the small number of categories, this system has proved useful in research and teacher training, in part because of the sophisticated manner in which the observation data are presented. The matrix technique, developed by Flanders, allows for the preservation of the sequential nature of the data which means that a reader can tell from looking at a matrix what preceded and what followed every verbal behavior of both the teachers and the pupils. This linking of behaviors into pairs, increases the power of the data, and this technique can be used to handle the data from other category systems.

One can read from a Flanders matrix not only how much a teacher criticizes the students, but specifically when he tends to criticize. That is, if he tends to accept narrow answers to fact level questions but reject students' own ideas, this would be revealed in a difference in frequency between the "student narrow answer - teacher praise" pair (category 8 followed by 2), as contrasted with the "student broad answer - teacher criticism" pair (category 9 followed by 7).

This system has been used in many different types of research, ranging from descriptive studies in which various teacher behaviors were correlated to pupil output measures such as attitudes, achievement, and measures of I.Q., to determine what teacher behaviors relate to various kinds of pupil growth.

Experimental research has also been done using the Flanders system, in which teachers were trained to role-play various teacher styles as determined by either "heavy" or "light" use of particular categories. In general, the results are similar in both descriptive and experimental studies. Indirect teaching relates more than direct teaching both to positive pupil attitudes, to pupil cognitive growth as measured by achievement tests, and to I.Q. scores in primary grades. The single most powerful predictor of pupil cognitive growth appears to be the teacher's use of accepting pupil's ideas (category 3).

The results are similar in both field and experimental studies. In general, the more the teacher accepts and encourages pupils in contrast to directing or criticizing them the more pupils seem to learn and the better they like it.

The Flanders system has been widely used in a variety of teacher training activities to provide teachers with a means of obtaining feedback about their own teaching behaviors, and the effects of those behaviors on the quantity and quality of student participation in their classrooms.

## OBSERVER RELIABILITY PROCEDURE

Reliability is established by having coders tally a tape together. Inter - and intra - observer reliability are determined by use of a modification of Scott's Reliability coefficient. The range of reliability scores reported by the author is .75 - .95.

## SUPPLEMENTARY MATERIALS

Computer programs:

Rippey (University of Chicago); Belanger (Harvard University);
Soar (University of Florida); Simon (Temple University);
Flanders (University of Michigan); Research for Better Schools, (Philadelphia, Pa.)
Northwest Regional Educational Laboratory (Portland, Oregon)

Flanders, Ned A. Interaction Analysis in the Classroom: A Manual for Observers. Ann Arbor: University of Michigan, 1966.

Flanders, Ned A. Four film strips and tape recorded sound tracks, Ann Arbor: University of Michigan.

Flanders, Ned A. Teacher Influence, Pupil Attitudes and Achievement. Washington, D.C.: Government Printing Office, U.S. Department of Health, Education and Welfare, Office of Education, Cooperative Research Monograph, Number 12, 1965.

Flanders, Ned A. Subscripting Interaction Analysis Categories, A 22 Category System. Ann Arbor: University of Michigan, 1966.

Amidon, Edmund J. and Flanders, Ned A., The Role of the Teacher in the Classroom: A Manual for Understanding and Improving Teacher Classroom Behavior. Minneapolis, Minnesota: 1967. (Revised Edition)

4 - Flanders

## CATEGORIES FOR

## THE FLANDERS SYSTEM OF INTERACTION ANALYSIS

### Ned A. Flanders

| | | |
|---|---|---|
| **TEACHER TALK** | **INDIRECT IN-FLUENCE** | **1.*** **ACCEPTS FEELING:** accepts and clarifies the feeling tone of the students in a non-threatening manner. Feelings may be positive or negative. Predicting or recalling feelings are included. |
| | | **2.*** **PRAISES OR ENCOURAGES:** praises or encourages student action or behavior. Jokes that release tension, not at the expense of another individual, nodding head or saying, "um hm?" or "go on" are included. |
| | | **3.*** **ACCEPTS OR USES IDEAS OF STUDENT:** clarifying, building, or developing ideas suggested by a student. As a teacher brings more of his own ideas into play, shift to category five. |
| | | **4.*** **ASKS QUESTIONS:** asking a question about content or procedure with the intent that a student answer. |
| | **DIRECT IN-FLUENCE** | **5.*** **LECTURING:** giving facts or opinions about content or procedure; expressing his own ideas, asking rhetorical questions. |
| | | **6.*** **GIVING DIRECTIONS:** directions, commands, or orders to which a student is expected to comply. |
| | | **7.*** **CRITICIZING OR JUSTIFYING AUTHORITY:** statements intended to change student behavior from nonacceptable to acceptable pattern; bawling someone out; stating why the teacher is doing what he is doing; extreme self-reference. |
| **STUDENT TALK** | | **8.*** **STUDENT TALK--RESPONSE:** a student makes a predictable response to teacher. Teacher initiates the contact or solicits student statement and sets limits to what the student says. |
| | | **9.*** **STUDENT TALK--INITIATION:** talk by students which they initiate. Unpredictable statements in response to teacher. Shift from 8 to 9 as student introduces own ideas. |
| | | **10.*** **SILENCE OR CONFUSION:** pauses, short periods of silence and periods of confusion in which communication cannot be understood by the observer. |

*There is NO scale implied by these numbers. Each number is classificatory, it designates a particular kind of communication event. To write these numbers down during observation is to enumerate, not to judge a position on a scale.

6

Abstracted from

# SUBSCRIPTING INTERACTION ANALYSIS CATEGORIES*

A Twenty-two Category System

**Ned A. Flanders**

*Unpublished document, School of Education, University of Michigan, Ann Arbor, Michigan, 1966 (mimeo).

# FLANDERS EXPANDED SYSTEM SUMMARY

### SYSTEM DIMENSION

| * | ** | |
|---|----|--|
| X | 19 | Affective |
| | 16 | Cognitive |
| | 6 | Work process (control) |
| | 4 | Behavior |

### TYPE OF COMMUNICATION RECORDED

| | | |
|---|----|--|
| X | 25 | Verbal |
| | 7 | Nonverbal |

### SUBJECT OF OBSERVATION

| | | |
|---|----|--|
| | 5 | Teacher only |
| | 2 | Student only |
| X | 19 | Teacher and student |

### DATA COLLECTION METHODS REPORTED

| | | |
|---|----|--|
| X | 18 | Live |
| X | 13 | Tape recording without tapescript |
| | 9 | Tape recording and tapescript |
| X | 13 | Video tape |
| | 1 | Handwritten notes |

### AUDIO OR VIDEO TAPE REQUIRED

| | | |
|---|----|--|
| | 9 | Yes |
| X | 17 | No |

### PERSONNEL NEEDED FOR OBSERVATION OR RECORDING SESSION

| | | |
|---|----|--|
| X | 17 | 1 coder |
| | 1 | Team of 2 |
| | 1 | 2 teams of 2 |
| | 9 | Tape operator |

### NUMBER OF CODERS NEEDED DURING CODING SESSION

| | | |
|---|----|--|
| X | 17 | No coder other than observer(s) |
| | 3 | 1 coder |
| | 2 | 2 coders |
| | 4 | 2 teams of 2 coders |

### CODING UNITS

| | | |
|---|----|--|
| | 18 | Category change |
| X | 9 | Category + time unit |
| | 6 | Content area change |
| | 3 | Speaker change |
| | 3 | Time sample |

### USES REPORTED BY AUTHOR

| | | |
|---|----|--|
| X | 26 | Research |
| | 12 | Teacher training |
| | 9 | Supervision |

\* Summary of information for this system

\*\* Summary of information for 26 systems

# FLANDERS EXPANDED SYSTEM

This system, an expansion of the original Flanders system, makes provision for more detailed data collection within eight of the original ten categories.

The expansion allows differentiation between superficial praise or acceptance and more genuine praise and acceptance in which teacher develops the student's idea or explains why he likes it.

The command category has been broadened to three sub-categories which form a work-process dimension ranging from statements in which unquestioning obedience is expected to statements which allow students to make alternative proposals for action.

The student talk categories separate student statements from student questions on both a broad and narrow level. Since students, like their teachers, rarely ask questions on anything other than a fact level, this category should reveal differences in students behavior in classes where the teacher is focusing on helping children learn to hypothesize and explore content in depth.

An additional six sets of "time use" categories are also provided.

## OBSERVER RELIABILITY PROCEDURE

No range of reliability scores reported.

## SUPPLEMENTARY MATERIALS

Flanders, Ned A. Subscripting Interaction Analysis Categories, a 22 Category System. Ann Arbor: University of Michigan, 1966.

## SUB-CATEGORIES FOR

## FLANDERS' EXPANDED CATEGORY SYSTEM

### Ned A. Flanders

| Level<br>Category | 1 | 2 | 3 | 4 |
|---|---|---|---|---|
| 1 | No subscripts for category 1. | | | |
| 2 | Superficial encouragement like "um hm" and expressions like "right," "good," etc. | Longer praise statements, often explaining praise. Most genuine. Kid really hears it. | | |
| 3 | Merely repetition superficial recognition of student's idea. | Student's idea is developed (or used) by teacher as seen by teacher. | Student's idea is developed by teacher in terms of other pupil ideas or compares to other pupil ideas. | Asks questions in levels 2 or 3. |
| 4 | Narrow factual questions, e.g., What? Where? When? and other questions emphasizing recall. | Broad, general, open questions which clearly permit a choice of response. Asks opinion | | |
| 5 | Narrow, factual focus. Restricted concepts & purpose. Low level in terms of reasoning. | Not level (1) and not level (3). | Negative and critical, but not "7". Disagrees without comment or explanation. | |
| 6 | Narrow commands to which compliance is expected and can be easily judged. | Explains his directions and how something is to be done. | Provides alternatives, reasons, invites students to help decide what must be done next. | |
| 7 | No subscripts for category 7. | | | |
| 8 | Student responds by making a statement. | Student asks question in "tight" format along teacher's lines of thought. | | |
| 9 | Student responses showing freedom of own ideas or simply taking the initiative in terms of talking. | Student asks questions showing freedom of student thought or initiative. | | |
| 10 | Non-constructive use of time | Constructive use of time | | |

# CODE SHEET FOR TIME USE CATEGORIES

## Purpose and Activity

| Code | Purpose |
|------|---------|
| 1.... | Long range planning |
| 2.... | Short term planning, new work |
| 3.... | Short term planning, done before |
| 4.... | Drill and review |
| 5.... | Evaluation--test or quiz--of product of work |
| 6.... | Administrative routine |
| 7.... | None of the above--catch all |
| 8.... | Not New Zealand |

| Code | Activity |
|------|----------|
| 1.... | Teacher in charge of class or part of class, incl. lecture and drill |
| 2.... | Similar to 1, except an audio visual device in use |
| 3.... | Teacher in charge, pupil or teacher reads frequently from book for class reaction |
| 4.... | Teacher in charge, works with individuals or groups--seat-work, supervised study |
| 5.... | Teacher in charge, unusual activity--games, dramas, songs, hukas |
| 6.... | Pupils in charge, teacher observes any activity |
| 7.... | None of above, miscellaneous |

## Formation and Freedom

| Code | Formation |
|------|-----------|
| 1.... | Total class |
| 2.... | Groups |
| 3.... | Individuals |

| Code | Freedom |
|------|---------|
| 1.... | Restrictive |
| 2.... | Can't tell |
| 3.... | Open |

## Task Set and Control

| Code | Task Set |
|------|----------|
| 1.... | Teacher set |
| 2.... | Pupil set |
| 3.... | Shared |

| Code | Control |
|------|---------|
| 1.... | Teacher Control |
| 2.... | Pupil Control |
| 3.... | Shared Control |

7

Abstracted from

# A SYSTEM OF TOPIC CLASSIFICATION
# CLASSROOM INTERACTION STUDY*

James Gallagher

Faye Shaffer

Sondra Phillips

Sandra Addy

Mary Ann Rainer

Thomas Nelson

*Published by Institute for Research on Exceptional Children, University of Illinois, Version 2, June 1, 1966.
Supported by grant #3225 from the Bureau of Research, U.S. Office of Education.

# TOPIC CLASSIFICATION SYSTEM SUMMARY

| * | ** | SYSTEM DIMENSION |
|---|----|------------------|
|   | 19 | Affective |
| X | 16 | Cognitive |
|   | 6  | Work process (control) |
|   | 4  | Behavior |

| * | ** | TYPE OF COMMUNICATION RECORDED |
|---|----|--------------------------------|
| X | 25 | Verbal |
|   | 7  | Nonverbal |

| * | ** | SUBJECT OF OBSERVATION |
|---|----|-----------------------|
|   | 5  | Teacher only |
|   | 2  | Student only |
| X | 19 | Teacher and student |

| * | ** | DATA COLLECTION METHODS REPORTED |
|---|----|----------------------------------|
|   | 18 | Live |
|   | 13 | Tape recording without tapescript |
| X | 9  | Tape recording and tapescript |
| X | 13 | Video tape |
|   | 1  | Handwritten notes |

| * | ** | AUDIO OR VIDEO TAPE REQUIRED |
|---|----|-----------------------------|
| X | 9  | Yes |
|   | 17 | No |

| * | ** | PERSONNEL NEEDED FOR OBSERVATION OR RECORDING SESSION |
|---|----|------------------------------------------------------|
|   | 17 | 1 coder |
|   | 1  | Team of 2 |
|   | 1  | 2 teams of 2 |
| X | 9  | Tape operator |

| * | ** | NUMBER OF CODERS NEEDED DURING CODING SESSION |
|---|----|-----------------------------------------------|
|   | 17 | No coder other than observer(s) |
|   | 3  | 1 coder |
| X | 2  | 2 coders |
|   | 4  | 2 teams of 2 coders |

| * | ** | CODING UNITS |
|---|----|-------------|
|   | 18 | Category change |
|   | 9  | Category + time unit |
| X | 6  | Content area change |
|   | 3  | Speaker change |
|   | 3  | Time sample |

| * | ** | USES REPORTED BY AUTHOR |
|---|----|-------------------------|
| X | 26 | Research |
|   | 12 | Teacher training |
|   | 9  | Supervision |

\* Summary of information for this system

\*\* Summary of information for 26 systems

# TOPIC CLASSIFICATION SYSTEM

This is a cognitive system requiring data collection by means of tape recordings which are then transcribed into tapescripts from which a team of observers code behaviors of both teachers and students.

This category system has three dimensions. The first dimension makes a division between content and skills. The second dimension is divided into three levels of conceptualization (data level, concept level, and generalization level). The third dimension is the logical dimension or style being used by the teacher or student (description, explanation, evaluation, expansion, activity and structure). This system determines whether a teacher is teaching in content or skills, on what level of conceptualization, and by what means he is teaching this level of conceptualization.

This coding system uses place value to aid in coding. All codes are tallied as three digit numbers. Thus, not only does the category number give the reader data, but its position gives data; for example, the three digit code 111, would mean category 1 in each of the three different dimensions, and each different "1" obtains its meaning from its place value in the three-digit code number.

The coding units of this system are topics, that is, the focus of class discussion centering on a given action, concept or principle. Each topic is marked off, named, and labeled, and must be at least fifteen typewritten lines of tapescript.

## OBSERVER RELIABILITY PROCEDURES

Two teams of two people divide tapescripts into topics and then reach consensus on naming and labeling. Each team does the same script independently and then compares judgments.

The reported range of reliability is 70 to 80% agreement between teams.

## SUPPLEMENTARY MATERIALS AVAILABLE

Gallagher, James, et al. A System of Topic Classification: Classroom Interaction Study. Institute for Research on Exceptional Children, University of Illinois, 1966.

Sets of tapescripts which have been coded and contain extended comments, are available from the author.

CATEGORIES FOR

TOPIC CLASSIFICATION SYSTEM

James J. Gallagher, et al.


The code is a three (3) digit number to correspond to the three dimensions of the classification system.

The first division is between CONTENT and SKILL and this would be classified and coded in the hundreds' column. The second is the level of conceptualization and this would be coded in the tens' column and the third is style which would be in the ones' column.

The codes are:

        1 - CONTENT
        2 - SKILLS

        0 - No determinable level (undeveloped topic)
        1 - DATA
        2 - CONCEPT
        3 - GENERALIZATION

        0 - No determinable style (undeveloped topic)
        1 - DESCRIPTION
        2 - EXPLANATION
        3 - EVALUATION - JUSTIFICATION
        4 - EVALUATION - MATCHING
        5 - EXPANSION
        6 - ACTIVITY
        7 - STRUCTURING

EXAMPLES:

A CONTENT topic at the CONCEPT level and in the EXPANSION style would be coded 125.

An undeveloped SKILLS topic at the DATA level would be 210 -- if the level could not be determined it would be 200.

A topic on STRUCTURING is called 007.

An ACTIVITY topic is coded 106 (content) or 206 (skills).

8

Abstracted from

# MULTIDIMENSIONAL ANALYSIS OF CLASSROOM INTERACTION (MACI)*

The Honigman System of Interaction Analysis

**Fred K. Honigman**

*Published by Villanova University Press, Villanova, Pennsylvania, 1967.

# MULTIDIMENSIONAL ANALYSIS OF CLASSROOM INTERACTION (MACI) SUMMARY

## SYSTEM DIMENSION

| * | ** | |
|---|---|---|
| X | 19 | Affective |
|   | 16 | Cognitive |
| X | 6 | Work process (control) |
| X | 4 | Behavior |

## TYPE OF COMMUNICATION RECORDED

| | | |
|---|---|---|
| X | 25 | Verbal |
| X | 7 | Nonverbal |

## SUBJECT OF OBSERVATION

| | | |
|---|---|---|
|   | 5 | Teacher only |
|   | 2 | Student only |
| X | 19 | Teacher and student |

## DATA COLLECTION METHODS REPORTED

| | | |
|---|---|---|
| X | 18 | Live |
|   | 13 | Tape recording without tapescript |
|   | 9 | Tape recording and tapescript |
|   | 13 | Video tape |
|   | 1 | Handwritten notes |

## AUDIO OR VIDEO TAPE REQUIRED

| | | |
|---|---|---|
|   | 9 | Yes |
| X | 17 | No |

## PERSONNEL NEEDED FOR OBSERVATION OR RECORDING SESSION

| | | |
|---|---|---|
| X | 17 | 1 coder |
|   | 1 | Team of 2 |
|   | 1 | 2 teams of 2 |
|   | 9 | Tape operator |

## NUMBER OF CODERS NEEDED DURING CODING SESSION

| | | |
|---|---|---|
| X | 17 | No coder other than observer(s) |
|   | 3 | 1 coder |
|   | 2 | 2 coders |
|   | 4 | 2 teams of 2 coders |

## CODING UNITS

| | | |
|---|---|---|
|   | 18 | Category change |
| X | 9 | Category + time unit |
|   | 6 | Content area change |
|   | 3 | Speaker change |
|   | 3 | Time sample |

## USES REPORTED BY AUTHOR

| | | |
|---|---|---|
| X | 26 | Research |
| X | 12 | Teacher training |
| X | 9 | Supervision |

* Summary of information for this system

** Summary of information for 26 systems

# THE HONIGMAN SYSTEM (MACI)

This system, based on the Flanders System of Interaction Analysis, focuses more heavily than Flanders on the emotional-personal aspects of the classroom. It has two categories focusing on teacher's reactions to and use of pupils' feelings and a corresponding student category allowing the observer to code when the students are talking on a feeling level. The system expands on the Flanders' categories of student behaviors and allows for separation between student's cognitive contribution and student's affective contribution. There is a category for student hostility so that the reader who looks at the data can tell immediately whether the student is exhibiting "Fight behavior" in the classroom. This category system also focuses on the teacher's means of involving students in the classroom and allows for determing whether students participate by being called on or whether the students volunteer to talk. An observation period of twenty to thirty minutes is recommended by the author.

This system has been used for helping teachers improve their teaching in micro-teaching settings.

## OBSERVER RELIABILITY PROCEDURES

Reliability not yet been formally established.

## SUPPLEMENTARY MATERIALS

Honigman computer program: The program builds a matrix and Data Summary Sheet. Data are analyzed on a dimension-by-dimension basis (Fortran IV).

Honigman, Fred K. Multidimensional Analysis of Classroom Interaction (MACI) Villanova, Pa.: The Villanova University Press, 1967.

Honigman, Fred K. MACI Abstract. Philadelphia: Department of Curriculum and Instruction, School District of Philadelphia, 1967.

Honigman, Fred K. Analyzing Teaching, An instructional Kinescope which explains the three-dimensional structure of MACI. Philadelphia: Department of Curriculum and Instruction, School District of Philadelphia.

# THE MACI CATEGORIES

SYMBOL   CATEGORY

## TEACHER BEHAVIORS

O    Performs Emotionally-Supportive Behavior
       Teacher behaviors that communicate concern for students' feelings.
Includes all teacher activity designed to boost student morale, show esteem, and
offer students praise for things not related to classroom tasks. May include the
teacher's observations or assumptions about students' feelings, but does not include his reflecting or commenting on emotions that students have actually expressed in the classroom.

a    Designates Student Performance "Acceptable"
       A cursory behavior which indicates that the preceding student performance
has been satisfactorily completed.

aa    Praises Performance
       A supportive behavior which exceeds a simple designation of correctness,
and rewards students for their performance.

b    Designates Student Performance "Unacceptable"
       A cursory behavior which indicates that the preceding student per-
formance has not been satisfactorily completed.

bb    Criticizes
       A harsh, punitive, blamelaying, guilt-inducing behavior. This category
includes teachers' self-justification.

c    Uses Students' Ideas
       Teacher behaviors that serve to integrate students' cognitive contri-
butions (expressed ideas) into on-going classroom processes. Includes repeating, analyzing, expanding, and building upon these contributions.
       This behavior is totally non-evaluative in nature.

©    Uses Students' Emotional Contributions
       Teacher behaviors that serve to integrate students' emotional con-
tributions (expressed feelings) into on-going classroom processes. Includes
repeating, analyzing, expanding, and building upon these contributions.
       This behavior is totally non-evaluative in nature.

d    Solicits: Response Optional
       Questions and directions that invite but do not require responses
(e.g., "Does anyone have any questions or comments ?").

e    Solicits: Response Mandatory
       Questions and directions to which responses are required.

dc    Seeks Expansion or Elaboration of Students' Contributions
       Questions or directions that seek students' elaborations of their own

SYMBOL  CATEGORY

## TEACHER BEHAVIOR (CONT')

(cognitive or emotional) contributions.

K     <u>Selects Participant</u>
  A signal to students to perform, such as calling their names or pointing or nodding to the selected participant. This kind of behavior contains no real content or description of the task that is to be performed.

L     <u>Lectures and Gives Information</u>
  All forms of verbal and non-verbal information-giving, including the teacher's expression of his own views and emotions. Included are all illustrations, demonstrations, and audio-visual techniques used to transmit information to students.

## STUDENT BEHAVIORS

1     <u>Gives an "Original" Contribution</u>
  Students' creative cognitive contributions that are relevant to the topic or solicitation at hand. Includes students' giving perceptions and opinions, asking questions, expressing preferences, and making inferences.

2     <u>Gives a "Pre-Structured" Contribution</u>
  Student contributions that follow along some pre-established line of thinking. Appropriate behaviors range from fact-giving and simple recall to following long and perhaps complicated (but clearly pre-established) processes in solving problems. In all cases, there is only one possible correct answer. This behavior - when correctly performed - is done strictly "according to the rules," and shows no real originality, creativity, or discretionary activity on the part of the student.

Ӿ     <u>Digresses; Gives a "Contextually Irrelevant" Contribution</u>
  Student contributions that digress from the scope or intent of immediately preceding behaviors (teacher or student), but remain within the realm of regular classroom activity. Includes all attempts to change the agenda.

①     <u>Expresses Feelings (Emotions)</u>
  Students expressing emotionality (joy, fear, anxiety, etc.) or communicating their feelings about other people. Does not include expressing "feelings" (i.e., giving perceptions) about nonhuman ideas or things. Clue to the emotional nature of a contribution may be taken from the content or tone of the behavior, or both.

3     <u>Misbehaves; Shows Hostility</u>
  Student behavior ranging from simple restlessness and various minor "misdemeanors" to outright fighting, violence, and acts of destruction.

## OTHER

S     <u>Silence</u>

M     <u>Miscellaneous</u>

Abstracted from

9

# AN OBSERVATIONAL SYSTEM FOR THE ANALYSIS OF CLASSROOM INSTRUCTION*

and

# CLASSROOM INTERACTION AND THE FACILITATION OF LEARNING: THE SOURCE OF INSTRUCTIONAL THEORY*

John B. Hough

*From Amidon and Hough (Eds.), **Interaction Analysis: Theory, Research and Application.** Reading, Mass: Addison-Wesley, 1967.

# HOUGH SYSTEM SUMMARY

| * | ** | SYSTEM DIMENSION |
|---|-----|---|
| X | 19 | Affective |
|   | 16 | Cognitive |
|   | 6  | Work process (control) |
|   | 4  | Behavior |

### TYPE OF COMMUNICATION RECORDED

| * | ** | |
|---|-----|---|
| X | 25 | Verbal |
|   | 7  | Nonverbal |

### SUBJECT OF OBSERVATION

| * | ** | |
|---|-----|---|
|   | 5  | Teacher only |
|   | 2  | Student only |
| X | 19 | Teacher and student |

### DATA COLLECTION METHODS REPORTED

| * | ** | |
|---|-----|---|
| X | 18 | Live |
| X | 13 | Tape recording without tapescript |
|   | 9  | Tape recording and tapescript |
| X | 13 | Video tape |
|   | 1  | Handwritten notes |

### AUDIO OR VIDEO TAPE REQUIRED

| * | ** | |
|---|-----|---|
|   | 9  | Yes |
| X | 17 | No |

### PERSONNEL NEEDED FOR OBSERVATION OR RECORDING SESSION

| * | ** | |
|---|-----|---|
| X | 17 | 1 coder |
|   | 1  | Team of 2 |
|   | 1  | 2 teams of 2 |
|   | 9  | Tape operator |

### NUMBER OF CODERS NEEDED DURING CODING SESSION

| * | ** | |
|---|-----|---|
| X | 17 | No coder other than observer(s) |
|   | 3  | 1 coder |
|   | 2  | 2 coders |
|   | 4  | 2 teams of 2 coders |

### CODING UNITS

| * | ** | |
|---|-----|---|
|   | 18 | Category change |
| X | 9  | Category + time unit |
|   | 6  | Content area change |
|   | 3  | Speaker change |
|   | 3  | Time sample |

### USES REPORTED BY AUTHOR

| * | ** | |
|---|-----|---|
| X | 26 | Research |
| X | 12 | Teacher training |
|   | 9  | Supervision |

* Summary of information for this system

** Summary of information for 26 systems

# THE HOUGH SYSTEM

This system, a modification of the Flanders system, reflects the author's interest in concepts of learning theory. The system contains categories which indicate, for instance, when a teacher is giving corrective feedback (feedback which enables the pupil to see that his behavior is incorrect and why), and pupil categories for elicited and emitted statements.

The system also reflects the influence of the theory of programmed instruction which places emphasis on pupils' practicing behaviors they have just learned and thus this system has categories which discriminate between different kinds of silence such as silence during directed practice activity, silence while students are thinking, and silence while the teacher is giving a nonverbal demonstration. In addition, there is a separate category for noise (when more than one person is talking or when the observer cannot hear what is happening) and nonrelevant behavior.

## OBSERVER RELIABILITY PROCEDURES

Scott's coefficient of inter-observer reliability is calculated.

The range of reliability scores reported by the author is .80 to .95.

## SUPPLEMENTARY MATERIALS AVAILABLE:

Hough, John B. "An Observational System for the Analysis of Classroom Instruction." In Amidon and Hough (Eds.) Interaction Analysis: Theory, Research and Application. Reading, Mass: The Addison-Wesley Publishing Company, 1967, pp. 150-57.

Hough, John B. "Classroom Interaction and the Facilitation of Learning: The Source of an Instructional Theory." In Amidon and Hough (Eds.) Interaction Analysis: Theory, Research and Application. Reading, Mass: The Addison-Wesley Publishing Company, 1967, pp. 375-87.

# CATEGORIES FOR
## THE HOUGH SYSTEM

### John B. Hough

<u>Indirect Teacher Verbal Influence</u>

1. <u>Affective clarification and acceptance</u> - includes the acceptance, clarification and recognition of students' emotional states. Statements which deal in a non-evaluative way with student emotions and feelings, i.e., fear, anger, anxiety, happiness, pleasure, etc., are included in this category. Such statements may recall or predict student feelings or may be a reaction to current emotional states of students. Statements of encouragement which do not praise or reward or do not deny expressed student feelings are also included in this category.

2. <u>Praise and reward</u> - includes statements with a positive value orientation directed at student behavior. Statements which praise or reward current behavior as well as statements of praise or reward for previous or predicted future behavior are included in this category. Also, included are statements which indicate teacher agreement with student behavior and thus by implication express teacher feelings regarding the value of the behavior.

3. <u>Cognitive and skill clarification and acceptance</u> - includes statements which show acceptance of or are designed to clarify student ideas or performance, but are non-evaluative. Statements which repeat or paraphrase what a student has said or are designed to help the student think through what he has said or done are included in this category. (Also, included are such statements as "um hm," "go on," and "OK," when such statements are not said with an inflection that connotes praise or do not represent habitual teacher behavior).

4. <u>Teacher questions</u> - includes questions to which answers are expected, but do not serve the function of other categories. Such questions may be about content or procedure or may ask for student opinion regarding content or procedure.

5. <u>Response to questions</u> - includes direct answers to student questions. Such answers may give information or opinion but must be responses which answer or are directed toward answering student questions.

<u>Teacher Direct Influence</u>

6. <u>Initiates information or opinion</u> - includes all statements regarding content or process which give information or opinion. Also included in this category are rhetorical questions.

7. <u>Corrective feedback</u> - includes statements that are designed to indicate the incorrectness or inappropriateness of behavior in a way that enables the student to see that his behavior is incorrect or inappropriate and/or why. Such teacher statements are restricted to cognitive or skill areas in which behavior can be considered correct or appropriate by definition, generally accepted convention or can be empirically validated as being a fact.

8. Requests and commands - includes directions, requests and commands to which compliance is expected. Questions which mention a student's name when the student does not indicate readiness to answer the question, are included in this category.

9. Criticism and rejection - includes statements which criticize or reject student ideas or behavior without reference to clearly identifiable authority external of teacher opinion or feeling (i.e., definition, common convention or empirically validatable fact). Also included in this category are sarcasm, and rejection or denial of student feelings.

## Student Verbal Behavior

10. Elicited responses - includes conforming responses to narrow questions, commands and requests and all responses which are highly predictable as a function of their having been previously associated with a specific stimulus or class of stimuli. Also included are incorrect responses to narrow questions, commands or requests caused by associative inhibition, responses such as "I don't know" and unison responses either verbal or nonverbal.

11. Emitted responses - includes responses to broad questions or requests which have not been previously associated with specific stimuli or a class of stimuli. Also included are statements of opinion, feeling, and judgment.

12. Student questions - includes comments which ask for information, procedure or opinions of the teacher or another student.

## Silence

13. Directed practice or activity - includes all nonverbal behavior requested or suggested by the teacher. Working problems, silent reading, etc. are included in this category. This category is also used to separate student to student interaction.

14. Silence and contemplation - includes all instances of silence during which students are not overtly working of problems, reading, etc. Silence following questions, periods of silence interspersed with teacher or student talk are also included in this category as are periods of silence intended for purposes of thinking.

15. Demonstration - includes periods of silence when chalk board, felt board, pictures, etc. are being used to present information or when a nonverbal demonstration is being conducted by the teacher.

## Nonfunctional Behavior

16. Confusion and irrelevant behavior - includes all occasions when more than one person is talking and neither person can be understood (excepting unison responses) or when the noise level in the class is so high that the person speaking cannot be understood. Also included in this category are confused behavior in response to a command or direction, irrelevant comments that have no relation to the purposes of the classroom and nonfunctional periods of silence.

Abstracted from

# THE TEACHER IN ACTION*

## A Guide for Student Observers in Elementary School Classrooms

**Robert Gilstrap**

# HUGHES SYSTEM SUMMARY

| * | ** | SYSTEM DIMENSION |
|---|---|---|
| X | 19 | Affective |
|  | 16 | Cognitive |
|  | 6 | Work process (control) |
|  | 4 | Behavior |

| * | ** | TYPE OF COMMUNICATION RECORDED |
|---|---|---|
| X | 25 | Verbal |
| X | 7 | Nonverbal |

| * | ** | SUBJECT OF OBSERVATION |
|---|---|---|
|  | 5 | Teacher only |
|  | 2 | Student only |
| X | 19 | Teacher and student |

| * | ** | DATA COLLECTION METHODS REPORTED |
|---|---|---|
| X | 18 | Live |
|  | 13 | Tape recording without tapescript |
| X | 9 | Tape recording and tapescript |
|  | 13 | Video tape |
|  | 1 | Handwritten notes |

| * | ** | AUDIO OR VIDEO TAPE REQUIRED |
|---|---|---|
| X | 9 | Yes |
|  | 17 | No |

| * | ** | PERSONNEL NEEDED FOR OBSERVATION OR RECORDING SESSION |
|---|---|---|
|  | 17 | 1 coder |
| X | 1 | Team of 2 |
|  | 1 | 2 teams of 2 |
| X | 9 | Tape operator |

| * | ** | NUMBER OF CODERS NEEDED DURING CODING SESSION |
|---|---|---|
|  | 17 | No coder other than observer(s) |
|  | 3 | 1 coder |
| X | 2 | 2 coders |
|  | 4 | 2 teams of 2 coders |

| * | ** | CODING UNITS |
|---|---|---|
| X | 18 | Category change |
|  | 9 | Category + time unit |
|  | 6 | Content area change |
|  | 3 | Speaker change |
|  | 3 | Time sample |

| * | ** | USES REPORTED BY AUTHOR |
|---|---|---|
| X | 26 | Research |
|  | 12 | Teacher training |
|  | 9 | Supervision |

\* Summary of information for this system

\*\* Summary of information for 26 systems

# PROVO CODE ANALYSIS OF TEACHING

The development of this system presents an interesting history of an attempt by a school district to promote effective teaching through a Merit Pay Study. Under the leadership of Hughes, teachers made verbatim recordings of classroom interaction which were later analyzed and grouped into behaviors which seemed similar until a category system of some ninety categories remained. These categories were then grouped into the "functions" that the behaviors seemed to perform for the teacher and class.

The system represents this author's interest in group processes in which the leader is the most influential agent both for setting the climate for the group, and for determining whether the power shall be shared by pupils and teacher or shall reside in the hands of the teacher alone. The main emphasis is on what the teacher does to set an optimal learning environment for the classroom group.

This is an affective system for which the data are primarily collected by means of a tape recorder, and then coded later. However, two observers in a classroom to record non-verbal behavior of teachers and pupils are also required. This system analyzes the functions that various sorts of teacher behaviors perform for pupils in the classrooms: functions that control or facilitate, functions that develop content by response (which would mean that the teacher works on helping the students understand the implications of what they have just said), functions that serve as personal response where the teacher is focusing on the pupils' individual feelings and needs, and functions of positive and negative affectivity which help set the climate for the classroom.

## OBSERVER RELIABILITY PROCEDURES
Inter-observer reliability score is reported as 81% agreement between two coders.

## SUPPLEMENTARY MATERIAL
Gilstrap. Robert. The Teacher in Action, A Guide for Student Observers in Elementary School Classrooms. Adapted from the Provo Code for the Analysis of Teaching, Provo, Utah: Provo City Schools Research Staff, 1961.

Hughes, Marie. Helping Students Understand Teaching. Salt Lake City: University of Utah, 1959.

Provo Code for the Analysis of Teaching, Provo, Utah: Provo City Schools Research Staff, 1961.

CATEGORIES FOR

THE PROVO CODE FOR THE ANALYSIS OF TEACHING

Marie Hughes

## Levels of Abstraction of the Code

The Code functions are abstracted at three levels. These groupings are named in rank of abstraction as follows:

I.  MAJOR FUNCTIONS: The first level of abstraction of the teaching act.

   1. Functions that Control

   2. Functions that Facilitate

   3. Functions that Develop Content by Response

   4. Functions that Serve as Personal Response

   5. Functions of Positive Affectivity

   6. Functions of Negative Affectivity

II. SECONDARY FUNCTIONS: The second level of abstraction of the act. This is a somewhat finer breakdown than the Major Functions and names the various ways in which the Major Functions occur.

   1. Functions that Control

      A. Structuring

      B. Regulating

      C. Informing

      D. Setting Standards

      E. Judging

   2. Functions that Facilitate

      A. Checking

      B. Demonstrating

      C. Clarifying

3. Functions that Develop Content by Response

    A. Serving as a Resource Person

    B. Stimulating

    C. Clarifying Content

    D. Evaluating

    E. Turning Questions back to Class

4. Functions that Serve as Personal Response

    A. Meeting Requests

    B. Clarifying Problems

    C. Interpreting

5. Functions of Positive Affectivity

6. Functions of Negative Affectivity

III. SUB-FUNCTIONS: The third level of abstraction of the teaching act. This is the finest breakdown and further describes or tells how the relevent Secondary Functions are used. Not all Secondary Functions have been found to contain Sub-Functions.

Abstracted from

# INSTRUCTIONAL FLEXIBILITY TRAINING*

11

Bruce R. Joyce

Richard E. Hodges

*From the **Journal of Teacher Education,** 17: (4) 409-15. Winter, 1966.

# JOYCE SYSTEM SUMMARY

|   |    | SYSTEM DIMENSION |
|---|----|------------------|
| * | ** |                  |
| X | 19 | Affective |
| X | 16 | Cognitive |
| X | 6  | Work process (control) |
|   | 4  | Behavior |

### TYPE OF COMMUNICATION RECORDED

|   |    |           |
|---|----|-----------|
| X | 25 | Verbal |
|   | 7  | Nonverbal |

### SUBJECT OF OBSERVATION

|   |    |                     |
|---|----|---------------------|
| X | 5  | Teacher only |
|   | 2  | Student only |
|   | 19 | Teacher and student |

### DATA COLLECTION METHODS REPORTED

|   |    |                                  |
|---|----|----------------------------------|
| X | 18 | Live |
| X | 13 | Tape recording without tapescript |
|   | 9  | Tape recording and tapescript |
| X | 13 | Video tape |
|   | 1  | Handwritten notes |

### AUDIO OR VIDEO TAPE REQUIRED

|   |    |     |
|---|----|-----|
|   | 9  | Yes |
| X | 17 | No  |

### PERSONNEL NEEDED FOR OBSERVATION OR RECORDING SESSION

|   |    |               |
|---|----|---------------|
| X | 17 | 1 coder |
|   | 1  | Team of 2 |
|   | 1  | 2 teams of 2 |
|   | 9  | Tape operator |

### NUMBER OF CODERS NEEDED DURING CODING SESSION

|   |    |                              |
|---|----|------------------------------|
| X | 17 | No coder other than observer(s) |
|   | 3  | 1 coder |
|   | 2  | 2 coders |
|   | 4  | 2 teams of 2 coders |

### CODING UNITS

|   |    |                      |
|---|----|----------------------|
|   | 18 | Category change |
|   | 9  | Category + time unit |
| X | 6  | Content area change |
|   | 3  | Speaker change |
|   | 3  | Time sample |

### USES REPORTED BY AUTHOR

|   |    |                  |
|---|----|------------------|
| X | 26 | Research |
| X | 12 | Teacher training |
| X | 9  | Supervision |

\* Summary of information for this system

\*\* Summary of information for 26 systems

11

# THE JOYCE SYSTEM

This system records only teacher behaviors along three dimensions: affective, cognitive and maintainance of the social system of the classroom. In part, this system was built as a feedback tool to help teachers broaden their behavioral repertoire.

For example, one of the dimensions of this system examines teacher sanctions for various kinds of activities in the classroom. One of these kinds of activities is "searching behaviors" in which children are encouraged to raise hypotheses or perform experiments. Although this kind of activity is widely promoted in educational psychology literature, it is apparently not a behavior which is natural to teachers. From the use of this system, Joyce suggests that unless teachers are specifically trained to encourage search behaviors in pupils, they will either ignore these behaviors or will negatively reinforce them. This seems to be the case even when teachers say that they believe that encouraging children's "search" activities is a good thing. Apparently practice and feedback are necessary to promote change in this aspect of teacher behavior.

This system also has a dimension for helping establish the standards which will be used in the classroom; the observer codes whether the teacher is setting the standards and determining procedures or whether the teacher helps the pupils determine what standards or procedures will be used in the classroom.

The author recommends that the length of an observation period be at least thirty minutes.

The communication unit in Joyce's system is defined as one verbal communication by a teacher on one topic to one audience for a period of time not to exceed 15 seconds, though it may be shorter. For longer communications, one unit should be recorded every 15 seconds.

The system can be used in any grade level and for any subject matter area.

## OBSERVERS RELIABILITY PROCEDURES

Reliability is established by correlations of frequency distributions within categories between two observers. The range of reliability reported by the author is .85 to .95.

## SUPPLEMENTARY MATERIALS

Joyce, Bruce and Hodges, Richard. "Instructional Flexibility Training." J. Teach.Ed. Winter, 1966, 17: (4) 409-15.

Joyce, Bruce, and Harootunian, Berj. The Structure of Teaching. Chicago: Science Research Associates, 1967.

# CATEGORIES FOR
## THE JOYCE SYSTEM

### Bruce Joyce

1. **Sanctions:** These are verbal communications which have a rewarding or punishing effect on the child. The sub-categories refer to the kind of student behavior which is rewarded or punished. There are five types of student behavior which may be distinguished.

> Search (S-1). Sanctions are coded S-1 when the communication rewards or punishes search or exploratory behavior by the child. For example, if the child raises a hypothesis or tries to perform an experiment and the teacher encourages him, the communication would be coded S-1. ("That's an interesting hypothesis.")

> Group Processes (S-2). A second type of sanction refers to inter-personal behavior or group process. If the teacher tells a group that they have been organizing themselves well, the behavior would be coded S-2, using a plus (+) sign in the grid. If the teacher scolds a child for being sarcastic with a classmate, the behavior would be coded "negative S-2," using a minus (-) sign in the grid. "Stop bothering the reading group" would be tagged as negative 2.

> Attainment (S-3). A third category of sanctions refers to the attainment of a concept or skill. Verbal communication which praises a child for spelling a word correctly would be coded S-3, using a plus (+) sign.

> Follows Directions or Rules (S-4). A fourth category of sanctions refers to those given for following directions or rules. A communication that admonished a child for doing the wrong assignment would be coded S-4, using a minus (-) sign. ("Mary is the only one to have finished on time.")

> General Support (S-5). This fifth category refers to generally supportive remarks by the teacher (or generally punishing ones). "You're the worst class I've ever had," would be coded negative S-5.

2. **Handling Information.** These are verbal communications in which the teacher is handling information or affecting the way the children will handle information in the course of a lesson. Three of the sub-categories refer to attempts by the teacher to cause children to handle information, the last two refer to direct informational communication by the teacher.

The sub-categories for Handling Information include:

> Asks Child to Hypothesize (I-1). A question or direction or lead from the teacher which is designed to cause the child to raise a hypothesis, justify a proposition, or otherwise classify data or search for relationships among data is classified as I-1. ("Why?" "What makes you think so?")

> Asks Child to Observe or Speculate (I-2). A question or lead from the teacher which asks the child to speculate or to make an observation of his own is classified as I-2. The child need not refer to the data, as in the case of I-1, but can make a personal expression, as a poem, picture, or other free production. ("What are some other ways of saying this?")

Lecture Question (I-3). Here only one answer is usually possible. Recall or observation can produce the correct response. Synthesis or analysis is not required to respond. ("How is also spelled?" "Who discovered electricity?")

Makes Statements (I-4). If the teacher makes a statement, that is gives information directly, such verbal communication would be coded I-4. ("The book was published in 1813.")

Makes Conclusions (I-5). This category is coded when the teacher gives a conclusion. The child might have done the thinking in the sense that the data are already present in the lesson. The teacher, however, makes the conclusion himself. ("The five causes of the Civil War....")

3.    Procedural Communications. Procedural communications are those which result in the establishment of classroom procedure or of standards of performance. The sub-categories are divided so that the critical element is whether the teacher is sharing the determination of procedures or standards with the children or whether she is making such determinations herself.

Helps Child Determine Standards (P-1). The teacher helps the children determine standards. A communication which asks the children to examine their behavior or performance would be labelled P-1. ("How can we help keep each group on the track?")

Helps Child Determine Procedures (P-2). The teacher helps children determine procedures. Communications of this type lead to cooperative planning or to taking into account child interests or information. Asking a group if they had completed their planning and were ready for help in research skills would be coded P-2. ("How can you find some more information?")

Determine Procedures for Child (P-3). The teacher determines procedures. Communications which specify the work to be done or which explain how it is to be done are coded P-3; e.g., the teacher calls on a child for recitation or other performance. ("Turn to page 16.")

Determine Standards for Child (P-4). The teacher determines Standards. Telling the children the passing score on a test or explaining rules of behavior would be coded P-4. ("This paper isn't neat.")

4.    Maintenance Communications. These are communications which maintain the physical or social system but which are not directly related to the substance of particular lessons. Three sub-categories are used:

Transition (M-1). This category is used for verbalism which help keep conversations going without interfering with the flow of information. For example, a child responds to a question. "MMMM....," responds the teacher, waiting for another child to respond or the original child to continue. ("Yes, perhaps so.")

Small Talk (M-2). This category includes conversational observations which are outside the main business of the classroom, although they may affect the social climate of the class or help the child express himself comfortably. Speaking for a child about his vacation trip, for example, would be coded M-2. ("I don't like this chalk.")

<u>Discussing Routine</u> (M-3).  Communications dealing with the physical arrangements in the room, such as the closing of windows, or communications in which the teacher is an agent of the school, as in announcing an assembly program or a fire drill, would be coded M-3.  ("Please open the window.")

Abstracted from

# MANUAL FOR IPI STUDENT OBSERVATIONAL FORM*

12

C. M. Lindvall

J. L. Yeager

M. Wang

C. Wood

*Unpublished document, Learning Research and Development Center, University of Pittsburgh, Undated, (mimeo).

# IPI STUDENT OBSERVATIONAL FORM SUMMARY

### SYSTEM DIMENSION

| * | ** | |
|---|----|---|
|   | 19 | Affective |
|   | 16 | Cognitive |
|   | 6  | Work process (control) |
| X | 4  | Behavior |

### TYPE OF COMMUNICATION RECORDED

|   | 25 | Verbal |
|---|----|---|
| X | 7  | Nonverbal |

### SUBJECT OF OBSERVATION

|   | 5  | Teacher only |
|---|----|---|
| X | 2  | Student only |
|   | 19 | Teacher and student |

### DATA COLLECTION METHODS REPORTED

| X | 18 | Live |
|---|----|---|
|   | 13 | Tape recording without tapescript |
|   | 9  | Tape recording and tapescript |
|   | 13 | Video tape |
|   | 1  | Handwritten notes |

### AUDIO OR VIDEO TAPE REQUIRED

|   | 9  | Yes |
|---|----|---|
| X | 17 | No |

### PERSONNEL NEEDED FOR OBSERVATION OR RECORDING SESSION

| X | 17 | 1 coder |
|---|----|---|
|   | 1  | Team of 2 |
|   | 1  | 2 teams of 2 |
|   | 9  | Tape operator |

### NUMBER OF CODERS NEEDED DURING CODING SESSION

| X | 17 | No coder other than observer(s) |
|---|----|---|
|   | 3  | 1 coder |
|   | 2  | 2 coders |
|   | 4  | 2 teams of 2 coders |

### CODING UNITS

|   | 18 | Category change |
|---|----|---|
|   | 9  | Category + time unit |
|   | 6  | Content area change |
|   | 3  | Speaker change |
| X | 3  | Time sample |

### USES REPORTED BY AUTHOR

| X | 26 | Research |
|---|----|---|
|   | 12 | Teacher training |
|   | 9  | Supervision |

* Summary of information for this system

** Summary of information for 26 systems

12

# THE LINDVALL SYSTEM

This unusual type of system is included because it is an example of the creation of an observation system to help assess the behaviors in a new experimental project. The project, Individually Prescribed Instruction, changes the structure of the elementary school primarily by means of utilizing self-instructional materials, and therefore the system reflects an interest in determining the self-directiveness of the pupil.

The system is used by a live observer, and records only the pupils' behaviors. The coding is done in two minute intervals.

## OBSERVER RELIABILITY PROCEDURES

Reliability has not as yet been formally established for this system.

## SUPPLEMENTARY MATERIALS

Lindvall, C. M., et al. Manual for IPI Student Observational Form. Unpublished document, Learning Research and Development Center, University of Pittsburgh, Undated. (mimeo).

# CATEGORIES FOR
## STUDENT OBSERVATIONAL FORM
## INDIVIDUALLY PRESCRIBED INSTRUCTION

### C.M. Lindvall, J.L. Yeager, M. Wang, C. Wood

I.  **Independent Work**

    A.  The student is reading independently
    B.  The student is working independently on a work sheet
    C.  The student is individually listening to a tape recorder
    D.  The student is independently viewing a film strip
    E.  The student is independently checking his work
    F.  The student is working with a language master
    G.  The student is working with a disc-phonograph
    H.  The student is using programmed material
    I.  The pupil corrects a test (makes corrections)
    J.  The pupil takes an individual test
    K.  The pupil corrects a study exercise
    L.  The pupil works with supplemental reading material
    M.  The pupil makes corrections on test
    N.  Miscellaneous

II.  **Teacher-Pupil Work**

    A.  The pupil seeks assistance from the teacher
    B.  The pupil receives assistance from the teacher
    C.  The pupil discusses his progress with a teacher

III.  **Non-Instructional Use of Pupil Time**

    A.  Pupil spends time at desk not working
    B.  Pupil waits for teacher or clerk to provide lesson materials for him
    C.  Pupil waits for prescription
    D.  Pupil goes to get materials
    E.  Pupil waits for papers to be corrected by a clerk
    F.  Pupil talks to other pupils
    G.  Pupil leaves room to get material
    H.  Miscellaneous

IV.  **Pupil-Pupil Activity**

    A.  Pupil asks assistance from another pupil
    B.  Pupil receives assistance from another pupil

V. <u>Group Activity</u>

    A. Pupil contributes to a group discussion
    B. Pupil takes a group test under supervision
    C. Pupil answers a question directed to him
    D. Pupil asks a question
    E. Pupil listens to a teacher lecture or demonstrate
    F. Pupil watches a film with the group
    G. Pupil listens to records with the group
    H. Pupil watches a performance with the group
    I. Miscellaneous

Abstracted from

# CODING TEACHERS' VERBAL BEHAVIOR IN THE CLASSROOM*

A Manual for Users of OScAR 4V

13

Donald M. Medley
Joseph T. Impellitteri
Lou H. Smith

*From **A Report of the Office of Research and Evaluation,** Division of Teacher Education of the City University of New York, Undated.

## OScAR 4V SUMMARY

| * | ** | SYSTEM DIMENSION |
|---|----|------------------|
| X | 19 | Affective |
| X | 16 | Cognitive |
| X | 6 | Work process (control) |
|   | 4 | Behavior |

| | | TYPE OF COMMUNICATION RECORDED |
|---|----|------------------|
| X | 25 | Verbal |
|   | 7 | Nonverbal |

| | | SUBJECT OF OBSERVATION |
|---|----|------------------|
|   | 5 | Teacher only |
|   | 2 | Student only |
| X | 19 | Teacher and student |

| | | DATA COLLECTION METHODS REPORTED |
|---|----|------------------|
| X | 18 | Live |
| X | 13 | Tape recording without tapescript |
|   | 9 | Tape recording and tapescript |
| X | 13 | Video tape |
|   | 1 | Handwritten notes |

| | | AUDIO OR VIDEO TAPE REQUIRED |
|---|----|------------------|
|   | 9 | Yes |
| X | 17 | No |

| | | PERSONNEL NEEDED FOR OBSERVATION OR RECORDING SESSION |
|---|----|------------------|
| X | 17 | 1 coder |
|   | 1 | Team of 2 |
|   | 1 | 2 teams of 2 |
|   | 9 | Tape operator |

| | | NUMBER OF CODERS NEEDED DURING CODING SESSION |
|---|----|------------------|
| X | 17 | No coder other than observer(s) |
|   | 3 | 1 coder |
|   | 2 | 2 coders |
|   | 4 | 2 teams of 2 coders |

| | | CODING UNITS |
|---|----|------------------|
| X | 18 | Category change |
|   | 9 | Category + time unit |
|   | 6 | Content area change |
| X | 3 | Speaker change |
|   | 3 | Time sample |

| | | USES REPORTED BY AUTHOR |
|---|----|------------------|
| X | 26 | Research |
|   | 12 | Teacher training |
|   | 9 | Supervision |

\* Summary of information for this system

\*\* Summary of information for 26 systems

# OBSERVATION SCHEDULE AND RECORD (OScAR 4V)

This category system has an affective, cognitive and procedural dimension which reveals how much of the time the teacher and pupils are spending on areas other than the content matter of the classroom. It has dimensions for analyzing both teacher and pupil verbal behaviors.

The system codes two sets of behaviors: interchanges and monologues.

The interchanges report only the teacher's behavior, making note of how the teacher starts an interchange and then how he responds to the pupil's answer. This technique retains some of the sequential nature of the data, and in fact has the coder build something similar to a Flanders Matrix as he codes. By scanning the finished coding sheet, the reader can tell immediately whether the teacher responded with explicit or implicit praise or rejection, responded neutrally, or ignored four kinds of pupil comments:

1) pupil questions,

2) responses to questions which refer directly to a previous pupil comment,

3) responses to questions which offer a pupil a choice of more than one acceptable answer or,

4) responses to questions which have only one acceptable answer.

This system, along with the Flanders System, has been used in an inter-observation system comparison to determine the differences resulting between Flanders and OScAR data. Cross system comparison is an important step for providing data necessary to create an optimal set of categories for use in varying settings.

The author recommends an OScAR observation period ranging from 30 minutes to a full class period.

## OBSERVER RELIABILITY PROCEDURES

Reliability is determined on the basis of correlation between scores rather than item-by item agreement of coders. The author reports a range of reliability scores from .52 to .69 for four visits.

## SUPPLEMENTARY MATERIALS AVAILABLE

Medley, D., Impellitteri, J. and Smith, L. H. "Coding Teacher's Verbal Behavior in the Classroom, A Manual for Users of OScAR 4V." From <u>A Report of the Office of Research and Evaluation</u>, Division of Teacher Education of the City University of New York, Undated.

CATEGORIES FOR

VERBAL BEHAVIOR IN OScAR 4V

D. M. Medley, J. T. Impellitteri, L. H. Smith

## I. STATEMENTS

A. <u>Teacher statements</u>--utterances which neither respond to nor solicit a response from a pupil--are classified as follows:

    1. AFFECTIVE. A statement revealing sensitivity to pupil feelings is classified as CONSIDERING. A statement criticizing pupil conduct is classified as RE-BUKING.

    2. SUBSTANTIVE. A statement containing no affect but referring directly to content to be learned by pupils is classified as INFORMING if it conveys a fact, generalization, or the like, or PROBLEM STRUCTURING if it sets up a question or issue to be solved.

    3. PROCEDURAL. A statement which contains neither affect nor substance is classified as DIRECTIVE if it contains a command or an instruction with the force of a command. A statement which does not clearly fall into one of the above categories is classified as DESCRIBING.

B. <u>Pupil statements</u>--utterances by pupils addressed to other pupils are classified as PUPIL STATEMENTS.

C. <u>Sequence.</u> If a teacher makes two or more successive statements which may be classified in the same category, all except the first are classified as CONTINUING. The first statement in a series of the same kind is classified as INITIATING.

## II. INTERCHANGES

An interchange is an episode in which a pupil says something to the teacher and the teacher reacts.

A. <u>Substantive interchanges</u> are those in which the pupil's utterance refers to content to be learned.

B. <u>Entries.</u> A substantive interchange begins with one of four types of entries:

    1. PUPIL INITIATED. The pupil addresses a statement or question to the teacher.

    2. ELABORATING. The teacher addresses a question to a pupil which refers directly to a previous pupil comment.

    3. DIVERGENT. The teacher addresses a question to a pupil which does not refer directly to a previous pupil comment, and which offers him a choice of two or more acceptable or "correct" answers.

4. CONVERGENT. The teacher addresses a question to a pupil which does not refer directly to a previous pupil comment and to which there is only one acceptable answer.

C. Exits. After the pupil has asked his question or made his answer, the teacher disposes of the answer in one of six ways, called Exits. Exits are first classified according to the information they contain about the correctness or acceptability of what the pupil has said.

If the teacher clearly indicates that what the pupil has said is correct or acceptable, the interchange is classified as SUPPORTED if praise or enthusiasm is shown, as APPROVED if praise is not given.

If the teacher clearly indicates that what the pupil has said is incorrect or unacceptable, the interchange is classified as CRITICIZED if disapproval of either the pupil or what he has said is expressed, or as NEUTRALLY REJECTED if no disapproval is expressed.

If the teacher makes some response to what the pupil says which does not clearly indicate whether it is correct (acceptable) or incorrect (unacceptable) the interchange is classified as ACCEPTED; if the teacher makes no response, it is classified as NOT EVALUATED.

Since these four entries and six exits are used in classifying them, it may be said that 24 kinds of substantive interchanges are recognized.

D. Non-Substantive Interchanges are those in which the pupils contribution does not refer to content to be learned.

1. TEACHER-INITIATED non-substantive interchanges are classified as POSITIVE or NEGATIVE according to the affective content of the teacher's question.

2. PUPIL-INITIATED non-substantive interchanges are classified as POSITIVE if the teacher supports, approves, or accepts the pupil's suggestion, and as negative if he criticizes, neutrally rejects, or ignores it.

Abstracted from

# THE COLLABORATION SCALE FOR THE ANALYSIS OF TEACHING: RESPONSIVE-DIRECTIVE DIMENSION*

George L. Miller

14

*Unpublished document, Lesley College, Cambridge, Massachusetts, April, 1966, (mimeo).

# MILLER-HUGHES SYSTEM SUMMARY

|  |  |  |
|---|---|---|
| * | ** | SYSTEM DIMENSION |
| X | 19 | Affective |
|  | 16 | Cognitive |
|  | 6 | Work process (control) |
|  | 4 | Behavior |

### TYPE OF COMMUNICATION RECORDED

|  |  |  |
|---|---|---|
| X | 25 | Verbal |
|  | 7 | Nonverbal |

### SUBJECT OF OBSERVATION

|  |  |  |
|---|---|---|
| X | 5 | Teacher only |
|  | 2 | Student only |
|  | 19 | Teacher and student |

### DATA COLLECTION METHODS REPORTED

|  |  |  |
|---|---|---|
|  | 18 | Live |
|  | 13 | Tape recording without tapescript |
| X | 9 | Tape recording and tapescript |
|  | 13 | Video tape |
|  | 1 | Handwritten notes |

### AUDIO OR VIDEO TAPE REQUIRED

|  |  |  |
|---|---|---|
| X | 9 | Yes |
|  | 17 | No |

### PERSONNEL NEEDED FOR OBSERVATION OR RECORDING SESSION

|  |  |  |
|---|---|---|
|  | 17 | 1 coder |
|  | 1 | Team of 2 |
|  | 1 | 2 teams of 2 |
| X | 9 | Tape operator |

### NUMBER OF CODERS NEEDED DURING CODING SESSION

|  |  |  |
|---|---|---|
|  | 17 | No coder other than observer(s) |
| X | 3 | 1 coder |
|  | 2 | 2 coders |
|  | 4 | 2 teams of 2 coders |

### CODING UNITS

|  |  |  |
|---|---|---|
| X | 18 | Category change |
|  | 9 | Category + time unit |
|  | 6 | Content area change |
|  | 3 | Speaker change |
|  | 3 | Time sample |

### USES REPORTED BY AUTHOR

|  |  |  |
|---|---|---|
| X | 26 | Research |
| X | 12 | Teacher training |
| X | 9 | Supervision |

* Summary of information for this system

** Summary of information for 26 systems

Abstracted from

# THE COLLABORATION SCALE FOR THE ANALYSIS OF TEACHING: RESPONSIVE-DIRECTIVE DIMENSION*

George L. Miller

14

*Unpublished document, Lesley College, Cambridge, Massachusetts, April, 1966, (mimeo).

# MILLER-HUGHES SYSTEM SUMMARY

## SYSTEM DIMENSION

| * | ** | |
|---|---|---|
| X | 19 | Affective |
|   | 16 | Cognitive |
|   | 6 | Work process (control) |
|   | 4 | Behavior |

## TYPE OF COMMUNICATION RECORDED

| | | |
|---|---|---|
| X | 25 | Verbal |
|   | 7 | Nonverbal |

## SUBJECT OF OBSERVATION

| | | |
|---|---|---|
| X | 5 | Teacher only |
|   | 2 | Student only |
|   | 19 | Teacher and student |

## DATA COLLECTION METHODS REPORTED

| | | |
|---|---|---|
|   | 18 | Live |
|   | 13 | Tape recording without tapescript |
| X | 9 | Tape recording and tapescript |
|   | 13 | Video tape |
|   | 1 | Handwritten notes |

## AUDIO OR VIDEO TAPE REQUIRED

| | | |
|---|---|---|
| X | 9 | Yes |
|   | 17 | No |

## PERSONNEL NEEDED FOR OBSERVATION OR RECORDING SESSION

| | | |
|---|---|---|
|   | 17 | 1 coder |
|   | 1 | Team of 2 |
|   | 1 | 2 teams of 2 |
| X | 9 | Tape operator |

## NUMBER OF CODERS NEEDED DURING CODING SESSION

| | | |
|---|---|---|
|   | 17 | No coder other than observer(s) |
| X | 3 | 1 coder |
|   | 2 | 2 coders |
|   | 4 | 2 teams of 2 coders |

## CODING UNITS

| | | |
|---|---|---|
| X | 18 | Category change |
|   | 9 | Category + time unit |
|   | 6 | Content area change |
|   | 3 | Speaker change |
|   | 3 | Time sample |

## USES REPORTED BY AUTHOR

| | | |
|---|---|---|
| X | 26 | Research |
| X | 12 | Teacher training |
| X | 9 | Supervision |

\* Summary of information for this system

\*\* Summary of information for 26 systems

# THE MILLER-HUGHES SYSTEM

This system is a direct outgrowth of the Hughes System. Miller grouped the ninety-or-so Hughes' categories along a dimension called Directive-Responsive, which focuses on the teacher's responsiveness to the pupils' train of thought as contrasted with how much he directs them to follow his plans. This system reflects Hughes' and Miller's concern with group processes and thus allows for collection of data about pupils' attempts to set procedures and standards for their own learning.

The category system has an affective dimension, which looks at how the teacher responds to pupils' attempts to develop the content and a social order dimension which looks at how the teacher reacts to the class' attempts to set and maintain expectations, decision making procedures, and so forth. The initial category focuses on how the teacher sets the stage for learning, whether he does it with or without giving the student some reason for learning the material or makes connections with previously learned material.

Another main category is how the teacher develops the content either by interacting with the students in a way which forces them to follow in his thought sequence, or by examining and clarifying their input into the learning situation.

Another category, measuring how the teacher gives information in the classroom, allows the observer to code whether the teacher gives the information as he sees the need for it or waits until students solicit information that they need. There is also an appraisal dimension focusing on whether the teacher appraises with or without public criteria. If the teacher evaluates (positively or negatively) with public criteria, the students not only learn whether they were right or wrong about the content, but on what criteria they were right or wrong, so that the next time they will have criteria for evaluating themselves.

The "maintaining social order" categories have been less widely used than the categories relating to the development of content categories.

The author recommends two or three twenty to thirty minute observation periods for collecting data.

## OBSERVER RELIABILITY PROCEDURES

Reliability is established when, before coding a tape script, the entire record is studied to get general perspective and to identify the concepts to be taught. If two coders are working, agreement is noted and disagreements discussed. If only one coder is working, sample records are coded twice, and all items coded for a record in both codings are counted. The formula for agreement is the proportion of agreement over total codings of both coders.

$$P = \frac{agreements}{agreements \ and \ disagreements}$$

The range of reliability reported by the author is 78 to 99%.

## SUPPLEMENTARY MATERIAL

Miller, George L. The Collaboration Scale for the Analysis of Teaching: Responsive-Directive Dimension. Lesley College, Cambridge, Mass., April, 1966, mimeo.

Miller, George L. "Collaborative Teaching and Pupil Thinking." J. Teach. Ed., 1966, XVII (3).

Miller, George L. An Investigation of Teacher Behavior and Pupil Thinking. Department of Education, University of Utah, May, 1964.

# TEACHING BEHAVIORS IN PUPIL-TEACHER INTERACTIONS:

## RESPONSIVE - DIRECTIVE SCALE

←————————————————————————————→

Directive                                    Responsive

### WORKING ON CONTENT OR TASK

#### Providing Focus

| | | |
|---|---|---|
| Structure initial without orientation or public criteria - SIWO | (initial why) or | Structure initial with orientation or public criteria - SIW |
| Closed initial structure - CIS | (initial how) or | Open initial structure - OIS or Structure turnback - STB or Stimulate - S |

#### Development

or

| | |
|---|---|
| Intervening structure (open or closed) - IS or Ongoing structure (open or closed) - OS | Clarify reflect  -  CR or Clarify elaborate  -  CE or Clarify examine  CX or Clarify generalize  -  CG or Clarify summarize  -  CS or Clarify testing  -  CT |

#### Giving Information Directly

| | | |
|---|---|---|
| Inform  -  IF | or | Resource  -  RS |

#### Appraising Effort

| | | |
|---|---|---|
| Evaluate without public criteria (positive or negative)  -  EWO | or | Evaluate with public criteria (positive or negative)  -  EW |

# MAINTAINING SOCIAL ORDER

## Setting Expectations

| | | |
|---|---|---|
| Set standard teacher edict - SST | or | Set standard, group - SSG |
| Admonish - AD | or | Set standard, universal - SSU |
| Verbal futuristic - V F | or | Meets request, makes arrangements - MR |
| Moralize - MZ | or | Interprets situation or feelings - ISF |

## Implementing Action

| | | |
|---|---|---|
| Regulate, closed, global - RCG | or | Regulate, with public criteria, open neutral - RWC |
| Negative response, personal - NRP | or | Meets request, routine - MRR |
| Inform appraisal - IA | or | Clarify personal problem or personal experience - CPR |
| Ignore request - IRQ | or | Does for personal - DP |
| Regulate self-teacher estimate of need - RS | or | Acknowledges teacher mistake - AM |

## Appraising Effort

| | | |
|---|---|---|
| Reprimand without public criteria or with a standard of teaching edict - RWO | or | Reprimand public criteria (standard universal or group developed) - RPC |
| Judge, punish, direction, just - J | or | Judge turn back - JB |
| Threat - T | or | Encourage - EG |
| Accusative - ACC | or | Solicitous - SOL |
| Support, just, steretyped teacher edict - SUP | or | Support specific, universal group developed, personal - SSP |

# FACILITATING

(These are neutral)

Regulate neutral, or sequential - RN
Checking, information, routine, involvement, - CH
Demonstrate - DM
Clarify procedure - CP

Abstracted from

# THE FLINT SYSTEM*

(Foreign Language Interaction System)
An Observational Tool for the Foreign Language Class

**Gertrude Moskowitz**

15

*Unpublished document, College of Education, Temple University, Philadelphia, Pa., 1966, (mimeo).

# FLint SYSTEM SUMMARY

|  | \* | \*\* | SYSTEM DIMENSION |
|---|---|---|---|
| | X | 19 | Affective |
| | | 16 | Cognitive |
| | | 6 | Work process (control) |
| | | 4 | Behavior |

**TYPE OF COMMUNICATION RECORDED**

| \* | \*\* | |
|---|---|---|
| X | 25 | Verbal |
| | 7 | Nonverbal |

**SUBJECT OF OBSERVATION**

| \* | \*\* | |
|---|---|---|
| | 5 | Teacher only |
| | 2 | Student only |
| X | 19 | Teacher and student |

**DATA COLLECTION METHODS REPORTED**

| \* | \*\* | |
|---|---|---|
| X | 18 | Live |
| X | 13 | Tape recording without tapescript |
| | 9 | Tape recording and tapescript |
| X | 13 | Video tape |
| | 1 | Handwritten notes |

**AUDIO OR VIDEO TAPE REQUIRED**

| \* | \*\* | |
|---|---|---|
| | 9 | Yes |
| X | 17 | No |

**PERSONNEL NEEDED FOR OBSERVATION OR RECORDING SESSION**

| \* | \*\* | |
|---|---|---|
| X | 17 | 1 coder |
| | 1 | Team of 2 |
| | 1 | 2 teams of 2 |
| | 9 | Tape operator |

**NUMBER OF CODERS NEEDED DURING CODING SESSION**

| \* | \*\* | |
|---|---|---|
| X | 17 | No coder other than observer(s) |
| | 3 | 1 coder |
| | 2 | 2 coders |
| | 4 | 2 teams of 2 coders |

**CODING UNITS**

| \* | \*\* | |
|---|---|---|
| | 18 | Category change |
| X | 9 | Category + time unit |
| | 6 | Content area change |
| | 3 | Speaker change |
| | 3 | Time sample |

**USES REPORTED BY AUTHOR**

| \* | \*\* | |
|---|---|---|
| X | 26 | Research |
| X | 12 | Teacher training |
| | 9 | Supervision |

\* Summary of information for this system

\*\* Summary of information for 26 systems

# THE FLint SYSTEM

This is a category system which is a direct outgrowth of the Flanders System and is used in similar fashion but with focus on the behaviors which are more commonly used in a foreign language classroom than in other subject matter areas. For instance, a behavior commonly used in a foreign language classroom is correcting the pronounciation of the students, and there is a FLint category for "correcting without rejection." In addition, there is a mechanism for recording whether the teacher or the child is speaking in the foreign language or using English. It has been used for training foreign language teachers.

The author recommends an observation period of 20 to 30 minutes in length.

## OBSERVER RELIABILITY PROCEDURES

Inter-observer reliability is calculated with an adaptation of the Scott coefficient. The reliability coefficient reported for this system is .85.

## SUPPLEMENTARY MATERIALS

Moskowitz, Gertrude. The FLint System, An Observational Tool for the Foreign Language (Foreign Language Interaction System). Unpublished document, College of Education, Temple University, Philadelphia, Penna. 1966 (mimeo).

## CATEGORIES FOR
## FOREIGN LANGUAGE INTERACTION SYSTEM (FLint)

### Gertrude Moskowitz

| | | |
|---|---|---|
| **TEACHER TALK** | **INDIRECT INFLUENCE** | **1.** ACCEPTS FEELINGS: In a nonthreatening way, accepting, discussing, referring to, or communicating understanding of past, present, or future feelings of students. |
| | | **2.** PRAISES OR ENCOURAGES: Praising, complimenting, telling students why what they have said or done is valued. Encouraging students to continue, trying to give them confidence in themselves. |
| | | **2a.** JOKES: Intentionally joking, kidding, making puns, attempting to be humorous, providing the joking is not at anyone's expense. Unintentional humor is not included in this category. |
| | | **3.** USES IDEAS OF STUDENTS: Accepting, clarifying, using, interpreting the ideas of students. The ideas must be reworded by the teacher, but still recognized as student ideas. |
| | | **3a.** USES IDEAS OF STUDENTS VERBATIM: Repeating the exact words of students after they participate. |
| | | **4.** ASKS QUESTIONS: Asking questions to which an answer is anticipated. Rhetorical questions are <u>not</u> included in this category. |
| | **DIRECT INFLUENCE** | **5.** GIVES INFORMATION: Giving information, facts, own opinion or ideas, lecturing, stating procedures, or asking rhetorical questions. |
| | | **5a.** CORRECTS WITHOUT REJECTION: Telling students who have made a mistake the correct response without using words or intonations which communicate criticism. |
| | | **6.** GIVES DIRECTIONS: Giving directions, requests, or commands which students are expected to follow. |
| | | **6a.** DIRECTS PATTERN DRILLS: Giving statements which students are expected to repeat exactly, to make substitutions in (substitution drills), or to change from one form to another (transformation drills). |
| | | **7.** CRITICIZES STUDENT BEHAVIOR: Rejecting the behavior of students; trying to change the non-acceptable behavior; communicating anger, displeasure, annoyance, dissatisfaction with what the students are doing. |
| | | **7a.** CRITICIZES STUDENT RESPONSE: Telling the student his response is not correct or acceptable and communicating by words or intonations, criticism, displeasure, annoyance, rejection. |

| | | |
|---|---|---|
| **STUDENT TALK** | | 8. **STUDENT RESPONSE, PREDICTABLE:** Responding to the teacher within a narrow and limited range of available or previously shaped answers. Responding chorally or reading aloud. |
| | | 9. **STUDENT RESPONSE, UNPREDICTABLE OR INITIATED:** Responding to the teacher with students' own ideas, opinions, reactions, feelings. Giving one from among many possible answers which have been previously shaped but from which students must now make a selection. Initiating the participation. |
| | | 10. SILENCE: Pauses in the interaction. Periods of quiet during which students are carrying out activities requiring no interaction. |
| | | 11. CONFUSION-ENTHUSIASTIC: More than one person at a time talking, so that the interaction cannot be recorded. Students calling out excitedly, eager to participate or respond. |
| | | 11a. CONFUSION-DISORDERLY: More than one person at a time talking, so the interaction cannot be recorded. Students out-of-order, not behaving as the teacher wishes. |
| | | 12. LAUGHTER: Laughing, giggling by the class, individuals and/or the teacher. |
| | | E. USES ENGLISH: Using English (the native language) by the teacher or the students. This category is always combined with one of the 14 categories from 1 to 9. |

Abstracted from

# THE ANALYSIS OF PUBLIC CONTROVERSY*

A Study in Citizenship Education

**Donald W. Oliver**
**James P. Shaver**

16

*Published by Harvard Graduate School of Education, Cambridge, Massachusetts, 1962.

# OLIVER-SHAVER SYSTEM SUMMARY

### SYSTEM DIMENSION

|  *  | ** |  |
|-----|-----|--|
|  | 19 | Affective |
| X | 16 | Cognitive |
| X | 6 | Work process (control) |
|  | 4 | Behavior |

### TYPE OF COMMUNICATION RECORDED

|  |  |  |
|---|----|--|
| X | 25 | Verbal |
|  | 7 | Nonverbal |

### SUBJECT OF OBSERVATION

|  |  |  |
|---|----|--|
|  | 5 | Teacher only |
|  | 2 | Student only |
| X | 19 | Teacher and student |

### DATA COLLECTION METHODS REPORTED

|  |  |  |
|---|----|--|
|  | 18 | Live |
| X | 13 | Tape recording without tapescript |
|  | 9 | Tape recording and tapescript |
|  | 13 | Video tape |
|  | 1 | Handwritten notes |

### AUDIO OR VIDEO TAPE REQUIRED

|  |  |  |
|---|----|--|
| X | 9 | Yes |
|  | 17 | No |

### PERSONNEL NEEDED FOR OBSERVATION OR RECORDING SESSION

|  |  |  |
|---|----|--|
|  | 17 | 1 coder |
|  | 1 | Team of 2 |
|  | 1 | 2 teams of 2 |
| X | 9 | Tape operator |

### NUMBER OF CODERS NEEDED DURING CODING SESSION

|  |  |  |
|---|----|--|
|  | 17 | No coder other than observer(s) |
| X | 3 | 1 coder |
|  | 2 | 2 coders |
|  | 4 | 2 teams of 2 coders |

### CODING UNITS

|  |  |  |
|---|----|--|
|  | 18 | Category change |
|  | 9 | Category + time unit |
| X | 6 | Content area change |
|  | 3 | Speaker change |
|  | 3 | Time sample |

### USES REPORTED BY AUTHOR

|  |  |  |
|---|----|--|
| X | 26 | Research |
|  | 12 | Teacher training |
|  | 9 | Supervision |

\* Summary of information for this system

\*\* Summary of information for 26 systems

# THE OLIVER-SHAVER SYSTEM

This category system was developed to determine teaching style in the teaching of controversial issues in social studies classes. It has two sets of categories, dynamic and static, for categorizing both teacher and pupil interaction during periods in which controversial issues are being discussed. The coding unit of this system is a single unit of thought.

This system has categories which reveal whether teachers and pupils are providing a basis of fact, description, legal principles, personal statements of values, and so forth, for claims that they make. In addition, there are categories which focus on the process of the discussion itself such as the relevancy of statements to the controversial issue being discussed or remarks which explicitly refer to the tactics being used by a discussant. The author suggests a minimum observation period of 25 minutes.

## OBSERVER RELIABILITY PROCEDURE

No range of reliability scores was reported by the author.

## SUPPLEMENTARY MATERIALS AVAILABLE:

Oliver, D. W. and Shaver, J. P.  The Analysis of Public Controversy: A Study in Citizenship Education. Cambridge, Mass: Harvard Graduate School of Education, 1962.

# CATEGORIES FOR

# AN OBSERVATION SYSTEM TO DESCRIBE TEACHER STYLE AND LEARNING OUTCOMES

### D. W. Oliver and J. P. Shaver

## Dynamic Categories

1. <u>Consistency-Inconsistency:</u> Statements that indicate explicitly or implicitly that the speaker is aware of a real or possible consistency or inconsistency within his own or another speaker's position. The inconsistency may be between two values, two facts, or two dimensions.

2. <u>Specification and Generalization:</u> Specification occurs when the speaker gives a specific statement to illustrate or support a more general statement. Generalization occurs when the speaker draws a more general conclusion from one or more specific statements already given.

3. <u>Qualifying:</u> A statement which deals with an implicit or explicit inconsistency by pointing out under what general circumstances an exception to a general principle is allowable or possible.

## Static Categories

<u>General Value Judgments:</u> Statements in which the speaker expresses a preference for a person, object, or position in the argument in terms of a general social or legal value, such as: personal privacy, property, contract, speech, religion, general welfare of the group, equality, justice, brotherhood, due process, consent and representation, etc.

<u>Specific Value Judgments:</u> Statements in which the speaker expresses a preference for a person, object, or position in the argument in terms of the specific case under discussion.

<u>General Legal Claims:</u> Statements in which the speaker asserts that someone has a legal right to do something, expressed in terms of a general legal principle, such as: rule of law, due process, equal protection under the law, constitutional restraints, etc.

<u>Specific Legal Claims:</u> Statements in which the speaker asserts that someone has a legal right to do something, but does not give a legal principle as a basis for the right.

<u>General Factual Claims:</u> Causal, descriptive, or predictive generalizations.

<u>Specific Factual Claims:</u> Statements describing specific events delineated in time and space.

<u>Source:</u> A statement or part of a statement describing the source on which a claim, definition, or value judgment is based.

<u>Definitional Claim:</u> A statement about how a word or phrase is defined or should be defined. It is also a statement of analysis by which several meanings of a single word or statement might be distinguished.

<u>Repetition:</u> A statement in which the speaker repeats himself or communicates something already stated in order to focus the discussion.

Case: A set of statements which describes specific, real, or hypothetical situations analogous to the one under discussion. Its main purpose is to elaborate the range of situations to which one might apply a value judgment.

Relevance: A statement which explicitly deals with the way a statement or group of statements is related to the total argument or to the specific point under discussion.

Debate Strategy: Ad Hominem or other remarks which explicitly discuss the tactics being used by a discussant.

Task - Procedural: A statement directed at controlling the immediate interpersonal situation; it assumes that everyone in the discussion is trying to do a conscientious job.

Deviance Control - Procedural: A statement directed at controlling the immediate interpersonal situation; it assumes that one or more people are violating group norms.

Abstracted from

# THE DEVELOPMENT OF A TAXONOMY FOR THE CLASSIFICATION OF TEACHER CLASSROOM BEHAVIOR*

M. Karl Openshaw
Frederick R. Cyphert

In collaboration with
Norman V. Overly
Edgar Ray Smith

17

*Published by The Ohio State University Research Foundation, Columbus, Ohio, Cooperative Research Project No. 2288, 1966.

# TAXONOMY OF TEACHER BEHAVIOR SUMMARY

|  |  | SYSTEM DIMENSION |
|---|---|---|
| * | ** | |
| X | 19 | Affective |
| X | 16 | Cognitive |
| X | 6 | Work process (control) |
|  | 4 | Behavior |

**TYPE OF COMMUNICATION RECORDED**

| X | 25 | Verbal |
|---|---|---|
| X | 7 | Nonverbal |

**SUBJECT OF OBSERVATION**

| X | 5 | Teacher only |
|---|---|---|
|  | 2 | Student only |
|  | 19 | Teacher and student |

**DATA COLLECTION METHODS REPORTED**

| X | 18 | Live |
|---|---|---|
|  | 13 | Tape recording without tapescript |
|  | 9 | Tape recording and tapescript |
| X | 13 | Video tape |
|  | 1 | Handwritten notes |

**AUDIO OR VIDEO TAPE REQUIRED**

|  | 9 | Yes |
|---|---|---|
| X | 17 | No |

**PERSONNEL NEEDED FOR OBSERVATION OR RECORDING SESSION**

|  | 17 | 1 coder |
|---|---|---|
|  | 1 | Team of 2 |
| X | 1 | 2 teams of 2 |
|  | 9 | Tape operator |

**NUMBER OF CODERS NEEDED DURING CODING SESSION**

| X | 17 | No coder other than observer(s) |
|---|---|---|
|  | 3 | 1 coder |
|  | 2 | 2 coders |
|  | 4 | 2 teams of 2 coders |

**CODING UNITS**

|  | 18 | Category change |
|---|---|---|
| X | 9 | Category + time unit |
|  | 6 | Content area change |
|  | 3 | Speaker change |
|  | 3 | Time sample |

**USES REPORTED BY AUTHOR**

| X | 26 | Research |
|---|---|---|
|  | 12 | Teacher training |
|  | 9 | Supervision |

* Summary of information for this system

** Summary of information for 26 systems

# TAXONOMY FOR THE CLASSIFICATION OF
# TEACHER CLASSROOM BEHAVIOR

This taxonomy of teacher behavior stemmed from an analysis of many existing category systems and resulted in a synthesis of the systems examined into a four dimensional category system. The four main dimensions of this system are: 1) source, that is, _where_ does the behavior come from (inside the classroom or out?), 2) the target (direction, considered either as an individual, a group in the class smaller than the whole class, the whole class, or an inanimate object, 3) the _mode_ (sign) of communication: speech, reading, non-verbal writing, etc., and 4) the function, or purpose, of the behavior.

This process of synthesizing the theory and category dimensions of many category systems is a necessary step in the development of category systems which can be widely used by researchers in different geographic regions in order to build a data bank of comparable material.

The authors suggest that a full period or entire kinescope be used for an observation session.

## OBSERVERS RELIABILITY PROCEDURES

Inter- and intra-team agreement is calculated. The reported range for intra-team reliability is 94-99% and for inter-team reliability is 49-87%.

## SUPPLEMENTARY MATERIAL

_The Development of a Taxonomy for the Classification of Teacher Classroom Behavior._
The Ohio State University, Research Foundation, Columbus, Ohio, 1966.

_Comprehensive Abstract_, The Ohio State University, College of Education, Columbus, Ohio, 1966.

# CATEGORIES FOR

## A TAXONOMY OF TEACHER BEHAVIOR

### M. K. Openshaw and F. R. Cyphert

A given encounter is categorized in each of the four dimensions. Each encounter may have shifts within the Sign Dimensions. Furthermore, a given behavior may be classified in more than one category of the Function Dimension. Any change in the Source and Direction Dimensions indicates a new encounter.

The instrument is presented in brief form below:

I. Source Dimension — Indicates the origin of an encounter.

   A. Orginate — The source of the behavior is undiscernible within the classroom setting.

   B. Respond — The source of the behavior is some discernible aspect of the classroom setting.

II. Direction Dimension — Indicates the target to which the behavior is directed.

   A. Individual — Behavior focused on one person.

   B. Group — Behavior focused on more than one person but less than the total class.

   C. Class — Behavior focused on the whole class.

   D. Object — Behavior focused on inanimate element in physical environment.

III. Sign Dimension — Indicates the mode of communication of an encounter.

   A. Speak — Behavior characterized by spontaneous speech.

   B. Read — Behavior characterized by oral reading of (printed) written matter.

   C. Gesture — Behavior characterized by purposive body movement.

   D. Perform — Behavior characterized by demonstration, nonverbal illustration, singing, etc.

   E. Write — Behavior characterized by chalkboard presentation, writing on a chart, or overhead projector foil, etc., but excluding drawing.

F. Silence – Behavior characterized by an absence of other signs.

G. Laugh – Behavior characterized by inarticulate sound of mirth or derision.

IV. Function Dimension – Indicates the purpose of the behavior within an encounter.

A. Structure – Set the context and focus of subsequent subject matter and/or process.

    1. Initiate – Introduce and launch an activity, task, or area for study.

    2. Order – Arrange elements of subject matter and/or process in a systematic manner.

    3. Assign – Designate required activity.

B. Develop – Elaborate and extend within an established structure.

    1. Inform – State facts, ideas, concepts, etc.

    2. Explain – Show relationship between ideas, objects, principles, etc.

    3. Check – Request information concerning understanding.

    4. Elicit – Solicit a verbal response that states facts, ideas, concepts, etc.

    5. Test – Conduct a written quiz or examination-- dictate questions, supply answers, without explanation.

    6. Reinforce – Confirm or sustain an idea, approach, or method through reiteration.

    7. Summarize – Restate principal points in brief form.

    8. Stimulate – Foster student involvement and participation.

C. Administer – Execute tasks of classroom routine and procedure.

    1. Manipulate – Arrange elements of the classroom environments, personal and physical. (Cause others to do something.)

    2. Manage Material – Provide or coordinate use of media, supplies, or materials.

| 3. | Routine | – | Request information regarding compliance with individual, class or school expectations (regulation). |
| 4. | Proctor | – | Monitor classroom during group activity, testing, student teacher performance, etc. |

| D. | Regulate | – | Establish and maintain interpersonal relations. |
| 1. | Set Standard | – | Impose or guide development of standards of behavior. |
| 2. | Support | – | Express confidence, commendation, or empathy. |
| 3. | Restrict | – | Reprimand, threaten, punish, etc. |
| 4. | Assist | – | Provide personal help; does for. |
| 5. | Inquire | – | Ascertain student involvement. |
| 6. | Monitor-Self | – | Recognize and interpret teacher's behavior. (Check own understanding.) |

| E. | Evaluate | – | Ascertain the relevance or correctness of subject matter and/or process. |
| 1. | Appraise | – | Verify by appeal to external evidence or authority. |
| 2. | Opine | – | Judge on the basis of personal values and beliefs. |
| 3. | Stereotype | – | React without stated reference to criteria or person. |

### Further Refinements

1. The addition of the Direction Dimension was found to be necessary when the system was checked against the paradigm theorized to contain the essential elements of teacher classroom behavior. There is a need for still further testing of this Dimension.

2. The Stimulate sub-category could be more critically defined so that some of those behaviors without observable relationship to the extension of the content or process of the lesson formerly coded under DEVELOP - Stimulate could more logically find a place under the REGULATE category.

3. There is a need to check the sub-category <u>Routinize</u> within the ADMINISTER category to determine whether or not it is adequately defined and sufficient to classify those administrative behaviors which proved difficult to code under the system of classification developed and tested in this study.

4. Considerable attention should be given to clarifying the distinctions between sub-categories of the DEVELOP category; distinctions between <u>Explain</u> and <u>Inform</u>, <u>Elicit</u> and <u>Check,</u> and <u>Reinforce-Explain-Inform</u> need special attention.

5. Because of the inability of the observers to be certain about the beginning and the duration of an encounter, a revision of the concept of encounter should be made to provide a more definite meaning.

6. Further refinements of the system of classification should make use of type-scripts of the oral behavior which have been coded to coincide with the categorization of the live or filmed behavior. In addition, a projector with a reverse and slow motion mechanism should be used for facilitating the resolution of differences of opinion of the observers.

7. There should be less reliance upon the timed-interval coding and more attention to the development of a composite picture based on different codings to be checked against a timed-interval observation.

Abstracted from

# SEQUENTIAL ANALYSIS OF VERBAL INTERACTION (SAVI)*

**Anita Simon**
**Yvonne Agazarian**

18

# SEQUENTIAL ANALYSIS OF VERBAL INTERACTION (SAVI) SUMMARY

**SYSTEM DIMENSION**

| * | ** | |
|---|----|---|
| X | 19 | Affective |
| X | 16 | Cognitive |
|   | 6  | Work process (control) |
|   | 4  | Behavior |

**TYPE OF COMMUNICATION RECORDED**

| | | |
|---|----|---|
| X | 25 | Verbal |
|   | 7  | Nonverbal |

**SUBJECT OF OBSERVATION**

| | | |
|---|----|---|
|   | 5  | Teacher only |
|   | 2  | Student only |
| X | 19 | Teacher and student |

**DATA COLLECTION METHODS REPORTED**

| | | |
|---|----|---|
| X | 18 | Live |
| X | 13 | Tape recording without tapescript |
|   | 9  | Tape recording and tapescript |
| X | 13 | Video tape |
|   | 1  | Handwritten notes |

**AUDIO OR VIDEO TAPE REQUIRED**

| | | |
|---|----|---|
|   | 9  | Yes |
| X | 17 | No |

**PERSONNEL NEEDED FOR OBSERVATION OR RECORDING SESSION**

| | | |
|---|----|---|
| X | 17 | 1 coder |
|   | 1  | Team of 2 |
|   | 1  | 2 teams of 2 |
|   | 9  | Tape operator |

**NUMBER OF CODERS NEEDED DURING CODING SESSION**

| | | |
|---|----|---|
| X | 17 | No coder other than observer(s) |
|   | 3  | 1 coder |
|   | 2  | 2 coders |
|   | 4  | 2 teams of 2 coders |

**CODING UNITS**

| | | |
|---|----|---|
|   | 18 | Category change |
| X | 9  | Category + time unit |
|   | 6  | Content area change |
| X | 3  | Speaker change |
|   | 3  | Time sample |

**USES REPORTED BY AUTHOR**

| | | |
|---|----|---|
| X | 26 | Research |
| X | 12 | Teacher training |
| X | 9  | Supervision |

\* Summary of information for this system

\*\* Summary of information for 26 systems

# THE SAVI SYSTEM

## Sequential Analysis of Verbal Interaction

This system was developed in order to allow for a generalized observation system that can be used with any group of any size dealing with any content, and not just a classroom group. Thus SAVI allows for the collection of data about the behavior of leaders and members of groups other than classroom groups and can be used to compare the effectiveness of the role of the teacher with the role of other leaders.

The system has nine major sets of behavior types. There are 28 major behaviors nested in these nine sets and as many more sub-categories available for special groups or analyses. SAVI can be used, to a limited extent, with as few as four categories: Defensive, Unsolicited, Maintenance and Topic or as many as five dozen. The category system has a polarized "maintenance" dimension focusing toward or away from the solution of affective inter-personal problems, and a polarized "task" dimension that focuses on the use which a group makes of information. This system can be used to chart group development through various stages of problem solving.

The system provides a conceptual and operational link between the affective and cognitive domains. Based on a theory that every statement contains a personal (affective) and topic (cognitive) component, the SAVI theory predicts that unless the affective message is unambiguous, and in the long run, supportive, the cognitive component of the message is unlikely to be used. The implications of this in the classroom are that a cognitive statement with a negative implicit affective message to the pupils will have less chance of being used by the pupils. Thus a teacher who takes the time to accept and work with the feelings of pupils, and who takes the time to let his pupils know that he accepts and understands their cognitive messages provides a climate in which pupils have a higher probability of using the teacher's cognitive resources.

Under this theory, observation systems which provide a measure of the teacher's affective response to pupil's cognitive messages will predict pupil achievement along the dimensions being positively reinforced by the teacher. Thus, if the teacher reinforces pupils' verbal high-level thinking, the pupils in that classroom theoretically should produce high levels of thinking verbally. This may or may not carry over to their written behaviors. If he accepts and works with higher levels of thought in their written work, then higher test scores may start showing up in the research literature.

The SAVI theory also postulates that only when a "climate of trust" is established in the classroom, will the use of a cognitive system predict those classrooms in which more learning is occurring. This would occur only after students can hear teachers' data-level comments such as corrective feedback as correction about their ideas only, and not as rejection of them as people as well. Once this stage is reached, the teacher with more skills in problem solving should produce more learning in the classroom.

## OBSERVER RELIABILITY PROCEDURES

A team of two coders code the same material independently. Percent of agreement is calculated. The reported range of reliability scores is 85 to 95%.

## SUPPLEMENTARY MATERIALS

Agazarian, Yvonne and Simon, Anita. Sequential Analysis of Verbal Interaction, Concepts I. Part I of a series of three papers presented at the annual convention of the American Association of Humanistic Psychology, New York, September, 1966.

Agazarian, Yvonne and Simon, Anita. Sequential Analysis of Verbal Interaction, Mechanics I. Part II of a series of three papers presented at the annual convention of the American Association of Humanistic Psychology, New York, September, 1966.

Simon, Anita and Agazarian, Yvonne. Sequential Analysis of Verbal Interaction, Applications I. Part III of a series of three papers presented at the annual convention of the American Association of Humanistic Psychology, New York, September, 1966.

Simon, Anita and Agazarian, Yvonne. Sequential Analysis of Verbal Interaction, Philadelphia: Research for Better Schools, 1967.

CATEGORIES FOR

SEQUENTIAL ANALYSIS OF VERBAL INTERACTION

Anita Simon and Yvonne Agazarian

SAVI category labels have been developed to classify the verbal behavior of any group.

Because these categories were developed for use in a variety of settings, it is not necessary

to use all of the categories at any one time. The present version of the system has a total

of nine classes of verbal behavior, expressed by twenty-eight major categories. Many of

these major categories are also further refined at a sub-category level. Under some cir-

cumstances SAVI can be used effectively with as few as four categories.

## THE TWENTY-EIGHT MAJOR SAVI CATEGORY LABELS GROUPED INTO NINE THEORETICAL CLASSES OF VERBAL BEHAVIOR*

| | PERSONAL | TOPIC | TOPIC & PERSONAL |
|---|---|---|---|
| AVOIDANCE | I. AVOIDANCE OF PERSONAL MAINTENANCE<br><br>Self Defense  SD<br>Hostile        H | II. AVOIDANCE OF TOPIC<br><br><br>Narrative  NA | III. AVOIDANCE OF TOPIC AND/OR PERSONAL MAINTENANCE<br><br>Everybody Ought      EV<br>Intellectualization  I<br>Defensive Joke       DJ |
| POTENTIAL APPROACH OR AVOIDANCE | IV. POTENTIAL APPROACH AND AVOIDANCE OF PERSONAL MAINTENANCE<br><br>Personal Sharing  PS | V. POTENTIAL APPROACH AND/OR AVOIDANCE OF TOPIC<br><br>Description              DE<br>Topic Questions         TQ<br>Topic Joke              TJ<br>Positive Reinforcement  PR<br>Negative Reinforcement  NR | VI. POTENTIAL APPROACH AND/OR AVOIDANCE OF TOPIC AND/OR PERSONAL MAINTENANCE<br><br>Opinion  O  Laughter  L<br>Quiet    Q  Proposal  P<br>Noise    N  Command  CO |
| APPROACH | VII. APPROACH TO INTERPERSONAL MAINTENANCE<br><br>Maintenance Question  MQ<br>Maintenance Give      MG<br>Maintenance Support   MS<br>Self Affirming        SA<br>Maintenance Joke      MJ | VIII. APPROACH TO INTERPERSONAL TOPIC<br><br>Response Narrow      RN<br>Response Broad       RB<br>Topic Clarification  TC | IX. APPROACH TO INTERPERSONAL MAINTENANCE<br><br>Topic Build       TB<br>Topic Reflection  TR |

*This organization of the nine classes is based on a suggestion by Peter Caffentzis.

# THE TWENTY-EIGHT MAJOR SAVI CATEGORY LABELS IN

## MATRIX FORMAT

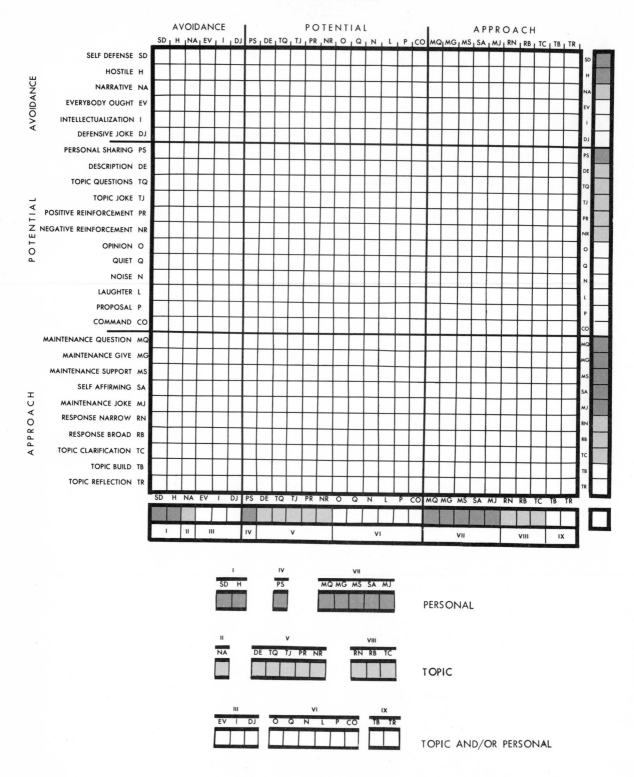

## SAVI CATEGORY SYSTEM LABELS

### I. AVOIDANCE of Maintenance

SD    Self Defense
H     Hostile

### II. AVOIDANCE of Topic

NA    Narrative

### III. AVOIDANCE of Topic and/or Maintenance

EV    Everybody Ought
I     Intellectualization
DJ    Defensive Joke

### IV. POTENTIAL Approach or Avoidance of Maintenance

PS    Personal Sharing

### V. POTENTIAL Approach or Avoidance of Topic

DE    Description
TQ    Topic Questions
TJ    Topic Joke
PR    Positive Reinforcement
NR    Negative Reinforcement

### VI. POTENTIAL Approach or Avoidance of Topic and/or Maintenance

O     Opinion
Q     Quiet
N     Noise
L     Laughter
P     Proposal
CO    Command

### VII. APPROACH to Maintenance

MQ    Maintenance Question
MG    Maintenance Give
MS    Maintenance Support
SA    Self Affirming
MJ    Maintenance Joke

### VIII. APPROACH to Topic

RN    Response Narrow
RB    Response Broad
TC    Topic Clarification

### IX. APPROACH to Topic and/or Maintenance

TB    Topic Build
TR    Topic Reflection

# SAVI CATEGORY AND SUB-CATEGORY LABELS

I. **Avoidance of Maintenance**

    SD    SELF DEFENSE

            SE    Negative self evaluation
            ES    Negative evaluation of self through others

    H     HOSTILE

            NC    Name Calling
            BL    Blame
            C     Complaining

II. **Avoidance of Topic**

    NA    NARRATIVE

            NF    Narrative Fiction
            NI    Narrative Information
            NP    Narrative Personal

III. **Avoidance of Topic and/or Maintenance**

    EV    EVERYBODY OUGHT
    I      INTELLECTUALIZATION
    DJ    DEFENSIVE JOKE

IV. **Potential Approach or Avoidance of Maintenance**

    PS    PERSONAL SHARING

            PO    Personal Orientation
            PH    Personal History
            CR    Credentials

V. **Potential Approach or Avoidance of Topic**

    DE    DESCRIPTION

            RT    Report of Thinking
            DH    Description Here and Now

                DHB  Description Here and Now Behaviors
                DHS  Description Here and Now Surroundings

            DT    Description There and Then

                DTB  Description There and Then Behaviors
                DTS  Description There and Then Surroundings

            DA    Data
            DI    Descriptive Instruction

    TQ    TOPIC QUESTIONS

        QB    Questions Broad
        QN    Questions Narrow

TJ    TOPIC JOKE

PR    POSITIVE REINFORCEMENT
          RIT    Ritual

NR    NEGATIVE REINFORCEMENT


VI.    Potential Approach or Avoidance of Topic and/or Maintenance

    O    OPINION

          E     Evaluation
          SO    Superlative Opinion
          IN    Interpretation
          SP    Speculation

               HY    Hypothesis
               AS    Assumptions

          WI    Wish

    Q    QUIET

    N    NOISE

    L    LAUGHTER

    P    PROPOSAL

          PI    Personal Intention
          SU    Suggestions

    CO    COMMAND

          ED    Edicts
          D     Directions
          OR    Orientation
          CN    Calling a Name


VII.    Approach to Maintenance

    MQ    MAINTENANCE QUESTION

          MQB Maintenance Question Broad
          MQN Maintenance Question Narrow

    MG    MAINTENANCE GIVE

          MGB Maintenance Give Broad
               FB    Feedback
          MGN Maintenance Give Narrow

    MS    MAINTENANCE SUPPORT

    SA    SELF AFFIRMING

    MJ    MAINTENANCE JOKE

VIII.  Approach to Topic

      RB   RESPONSE BROAD

      RN   RESPONSE NARROW

      TC   TOPIC CLARIFICATION

          TCQ  Topic Clarification Questions

IX.  Approach to Topic and/or Maintenance

      TB   TOPIC BUILD

      TR   TOPIC REFLECTION

          TRH Topic Reflection Here and Now
          TRT Topic Reflection There and Then

I. <u>Avoidance of Maintenance</u>

    \*SD  SELF DEFENSE - Negative criticism or apology for self; self deni-
           gration

        SE - <u>Negative self-evaluation</u>: Self-justification or self-apology,
           excuses and apologies that are not solicited and contain de-
           fensive feeling. Negative self-evaluations, suggestions or
           proposals about self, one's thinking or one's feeling.

             Examples:   I didn't mean to ...

                              I'm stupid!

                              My hair looks a mess.

                              I shouldn't have cried like that.

        ES - <u>Negative evaluation of self through others</u>:
           Reading another's neutral remark as a derogatory statement
           about self. Taking a generalization personally; talking as if
           someone is thinking or talking critically about self without
           evidence.

             Examples:   (In reply to statement: All blondes are dumb.
                              The reply (by a blonde): Well, I'm not dumb!

    \*H    HOSTILE - Negative criticism of others, of objects, direct verbal
              attack, sarcastic opinions and questions. Attacking ques-
              tions, indignant questions directly denigrating a person.

             Examples:   Boy, are you stupid!

                              Do you always wipe your mouth on the
                                 back of your hand?

                              You behaved like a fool!

           Denigrating opinion of material being worked with or mode
           of working, whether solicited or unsolicited.

             Example:    This is a stupid course.

        NC - <u>Name Calling</u>

             Example:    Idiot!

        BL - <u>Blame</u>: Personal, accusative value judgements of group
            members. Scapegoating.

             Examples:   It's your fault!

                                Look what you have done to me!

                                It's the fault of the guy in the White House.

        C  - <u>Complaining</u>: Expressions of resentment, implication of
            "that's not fair."

\*Main Categories

I. Avoidance of Maintenance (Continued)

Example: I never get to do anything I want to like my sisters do.

Indirectly blameful narrative. Implied: that the speaker is helpless to do anything about the situation. Indirect criticism of past events. Whining. Narrative information that implies things ought to be different or should have been different.

Examples: Bobby has three cookies and I only have two!

Sis can stay up later than I can. That's not fair!

My husband never does anything that I want to do!

## II.    Avoidance of Topic

*NA    NARRATIVE    –    Anecdotes, recitation of the details of a story.  Personal information or experience that has occurred outside the group.

> Examples:    I remember last September at the convention . . .
>
> Last weekend my husband and I . . .
>
> We went to Expo this summer . . .

NF    –    Narrative Fiction:    Fiction presented as fact.  Fantasizing how things could be, and presenting them as if they already had reality.

> Example:    Suppose I take this new soda product of ours and I test its acceptance in all the supermarkets.  Give everybody samples.  Now, everyone who tastes it just loves it and I'm selling thousands and thousands of cases each day...well, see there the company is already making millions.

NI    –    Narrative Information:  Nonpersonal stories or anecdotes.

> Example:    Have you heard the story ... ?

NP    –    Narrative Personal:  Personal anecdotes not invested with feeling or significance for the person, or direct relationship to topic.

> Example:    A funny thing happened to me on the way here...

*Main Category

## III. Avoidance of Topic and/or Maintenance

**\*EV EVERYBODY OUGHT** - Dogmatic value judgments that imply general prescriptions of what everybody ought to know or what everybody ought to be doing.

> Example:     Everybody ought to know that.

**\*I INTELLECTUALIZATION** - Analysis of a problem in purely intellectual terms to the neglect or exclusion of feelings or practical considerations. Jargon that is not shared by the group.

> Example:     I have an oedipus complex.

**\*DJ DEFENSIVE JOKE** - Jokes made at the expense of a person, self, or the work.

> Example:     Hi, I'm Hostile Harry!

## IV. Potential Approach or Avoidance of Maintenance

**\*PS PERSONAL SHARING** - Personal information about likes, dislikes, happenings or events that are "close" to the person; personal descriptions of "how I feel - what I want" in relation to the topic or task.

> Examples:     I am confused at the moment.
>
> I never have been able to do math at school...

**PO - Personal Orientation:** Personal orientation to the topic or the group (NOT personal sharing of feeling).

> Example:     I am confused at the moment.

**PH - Personal History:** Personal history invested with feeling or significance for the person.

> Example:     I was the youngest of five and had everything handed down.

**CR - Credentials:** Personal credentials like name, address, place of work and status.

\*Main Categories

# V. Potential Approach or Avoidance of Topic

**\*DE** **DESCRIPTION** - Description of condition of objects, activities, behaviors or thinking.

**RT** **Report of Thinking**: Report of a person's thinking about a topic; why he holds an opinion; reasons for a proposal; additional information clarifying his own question or answer, or thinking.

> Examples: I have been wondering about that, and last night I thought that if we had a conceptual framework that included both factors . . . . .
>
> We ought to decide today, because if we leave it till tomorrow John won't be here.

**DH** **Description Here and Now**: Observations of processes of behavior. Unsolicited feedback of how I perceive a person behaving. Description of physical environment.

**DHB** **Description of Behaviors**: Description of behavioral process in group.

> Example: Every time John speaks, Dave contradicts him.

**DHS** **Description of Surroundings**: Observations about physical environment.

> Examples: There are six chairs in this room.
>
> It is raining outside.

**DT** **Description There and Then**: Observations of past processes of behavior, or past physical environment. Conditions of objects and activities or environment.

**DTB** **Description There and Then Behaviors**: Description of past behavior external to the group.

> Example: I broke your typewriter.

**DTS** **Description There and Then Surroundings**: Description of past surroundings.

> Example: Yesterday there were six people in the committee meeting.

**DA** **Data**: Something given or admitted especially as a basis for reasoning or inference. Factual information used as a basis especially for discussion or decision. Information with an empirical basis that is introduced by a group member from a source outside the group.

> Examples: As Hempill says: "Leadership is a function of clarity of goal."
>
> The federal government is spending 5 billions of dollars for scientific research.

\*Main Category

## V. Potential Approach or Avoidance of Topic  (Continued)

Note:  The accuracy of the data is not judged, data is categorized by criteria.

Example:    President Johnson has six toes on each foot.

DI    Descriptive Instructions:  Instructions on how to do; guidance, supervision of action or conduct.

Example:    This is how one uses a typewriter.

*TQ    TOPIC QUESTIONS - Questions of a non-personal nature.

QB    Question Broad:  Broad questions of a general non-personal nature.

Example:    What do you think would happen if...?

QN    Question Narrow:  Specific non-personal questions, which can usually be answered by a yes or no, or a one or two word factual answer.

Examples:    Where is the United Nations Building?

What date did Columbus discover America?

*TJ    TOPIC JOKE - Something said to provoke laughter; jests, puns about the topic at hand or the situation in which the discussion is taking place.  Non-defensive, non-maintenance.  Does not include anecdotes from personal life.

Example:    I'm not going to allow my role as temporary chairman keep me from expressing my opinions.

*PR    POSITIVE REINFORCEMENT - Agreement.  Gives encouragement for speaker to continue along his same line of conversation, but gives no other information than the listener has heard the message and agrees.

Examples:    Right.

I agree.

Mmmm-hmmm.

Okay.

Yes, I guess so.

I suppose.

You're right.

*Main Categories

RIT -  Ritual:  Formula, polite stereotypic interchanges - without feeling.

Examples:  Thank you.

How are you?

Good to see you.

Good of you to come.

I guess so.

*NR  NEGATIVE REINFORCEMENT - Disagreement.  Tends to discourage the discussed topic and tends to change the direction of the conversation away from the subject discussed or to channel it in a different direction.

Examples:  I don't agree.

No, I don't think so.

It wasn't like that.

I don't know.

# VI. Potential Approach or Avoidance of Topic and/or Maintenance

*O   OPINION - Conclusions unsupported by facts. Judgments, appraisals, interpretations, speculations, assumptions about a topic. Implies a conclusion, voiced without making explicit the basis from which it was derived.

> Examples:  Teachers' effectiveness can be improved by group dynamics training.
>
> You look better in red than blue.

E   Evaluation:  Statements which contain the speaker's value judgment about something external to the group.

> Example:   Roosevelt was a good president.

SO   Superlative Opinion:  Opinions containing extravagant or evaluative superlatives but which do not imply a generalized prescription.

> Examples:  The NASA Organization is the best organization I have ever heard of.
>
> Our lawn is the greenest one in town.

IN   Interpretation:  Bringing out the meaning of, or giving one's own conception of a statement; explaining the meaning of, making understandable, or elucidating a statement.

> Example:   I think you are really talking about our staffing problem.

SP   Speculation:  To reflect or review something idly or casually and often inconclusively.

> Examples:  I wonder what would happen if I did this.
>
> Perhaps if . . . .
>
> Suppose we were to do it this way.

HY - Hypothesis:  A tentative assumption made in order to draw out and test its logical or empirical consequences.  (Potentially testable)

An hypothesis implies insufficiency of presently attainable evidence and therefore a tentative explanation.  An interpretation of a practical situation or condition taken as the ground for action.

> Examples:  If I stay in the sun any longer, I may get sunburned.
>
> If I eat more candy, I may get more cavities.

AS - Assumptions:  The supposition something is true or a fact or statement taken for granted.

> Example:   I know we all want to thank Mr. Bore for his generous two-hour speech on . . .

*Main Category

## VI. Potential Approach or Avoidance of Topic and/or Maintenance

WI   <u>Wish:</u>  A desire or longing without overt attempt to attain.

Examples:   I wish we could ...

If only you would ...

I wish it hadn't happened.

*Q   QUIET - Silence in the group.

*N   NOISE - More than one person speaking in the group.  Too much noise for the coder to hear what is happening.

*L   LAUGHTER - Laughter by members of the group.

*P   PROPOSAL - The act of putting forward or stating something for consideration.  Influence attempts.

Example:   Let's go back to work.

PI   <u>Personal Intention:</u>  Statements of what one intends to do. (For statements of personal self-assertion, see the definition for MS.  For statements of where I "stand" in relation to the topic being discussed, see the definition for PS.)

Example:   I'd like to talk to that point.

SU   <u>Suggestions:</u>  To imply as a possibility.

Example:   Perhaps it could be done this way.

*CO   COMMAND - To order or direct another's behavior.

ED   <u>Edicts:</u>  An official public proclamation having the force of law; an order.

Examples:   Follow the manual exactly.

Stop!

D   <u>Directions:</u>  Act of directing or aiming another's behavior.

Example:   Sue, would you like to read next?

OR   <u>Orientation:</u>  What will be happening.
Procedures - When and how it will be happening to the group.

CN   <u>Calling a Name:</u>  Call the name of a person to indicate that he is to follow the behavior prescribed.

*Main Categories

# VII. Approach to Maintenance

**\*MQ   MAINTENANCE QUESTION** - Questions which help a person clarify his feelings about matters very meaningful to him.

**MQB   Maintenance Question Broad:** Questions which help a person clarify his feelings about matters very meaningful to him; general questions.

Example:   (said to a person who looks unhappy): Would you like to talk about what's happening to you?

**MQN   Maintenance Question Narrow:** Questions which help a person clarify his feelings about matters very meaningful to him; questions which elicit a yes, no, or one-word answer.

Example:   Are you feeling better today?

**\*MG   MAINTENANCE GIVE** - Giving personal information about oneself either in response to a question or as an unsolicited remark.

**MGB   Maintenance Give Broad:** Giving personal information about oneself either in response to a question or as an unsolicited remark. An MGB is a general personal answer.

Example:   I feel happiest when I am free to say what I really feel.

**FB   Feedback:** A direct request or unsolicited report (perceptual) of the result of one's behavior upon other persons.

Examples:   Does it bother you when I raise my voice?

Only when I think you're angry with me.

**MGN   Maintenance Give Narrow:** Giving personal information about oneself, either in response to a question or as an unsolicited remark. It is a specific answer, frequently a yes or no.

Example:   I'm feeling much better now.

**\*MS   MAINTENANCE SUPPORT** - To strengthen by additional assistance, material or support. Remarks that emotionally support a person and inform him the "MS speaker" understands how the listener feels.

Examples:   I think I know how you feel...the same thing happened to me.

Right now you're feeling angry.

\*Main Categories

*SA     SELF AFFIRMING - Statements of a self-declarative and self-affirming nature supporting one's stand or one's self without being defensive or hostile.

         Example:     I think I have said enough about the subject and it is all I intend to say.

                     I do not intend to buy your magazines.

*MJ     MAINTENANCE JOKE - Something said or done to provoke laughter. Maintenance jokes are good-natured jests supporting another person or the group. They are non-defensive, non-hostile, non-critical.

         Example:     I feel so good about this group, I may never leave -- you'll have to start charging me rent.

*Main Categories

VIII.   Approach to Topic

*RB    RESPONSE BROAD -   Answers to questions which require a person to state an opinion, make inferences, make an evaluation, state a relationship between facts or sets of facts; answers to questions to which there are no right or wrong answers (evaluative or divergent question).

Examples:   (In answer to questions:)

I feel group dynamics training can be helpful to supervisors because...

If there were water on the moon, then...

*RN    RESPONSE NARROW -   Answers to questions which are right or wrong, or to which there is only one answer or a limited number of answers.   Factual answers.

Example:   (What time did the meeting start?)

The meeting started at 8:30

*TC    TOPIC CLARIFICATION - Clarification, expansion, or enlargement of subject material being worked with immediately.

Example:    That is, I think we should invite new members, but first we should form a screening committee to do initial interviewing.

TQC    Topic Clarification Questions:  Questions that ask directly for clarification, expansion, or enlargement of subject matter being worked with.

Example:    "...Freud?  Anna or Sigmund?"

*Main Categories

# IX. Approach to Topic and/or Maintenance

**\*TB    TOPIC BUILD -**  To build on, or add to, another's idea. Immediate addition of a new and very closely related idea to one just mentioned. Agreement with the person's thought is implied.

> Examples:    (1st person)    I think we should work on this problem...
>
> (2nd person)    ...and work on it hard.
>
> (1st person)    This article needs to be revised...
>
> (2nd person)    ...and proofread.

**\*TR    TOPIC REFLECTION -**  Quotation or paraphrase of something said within the group. Indicates to the group that the speaker has attempted to hear the original message. In tallying, accuracy of the statement is not judged; it is the attempt, not the content that is tallied.

> Examples:    I heard you say this job is difficult.
>
> When our group met last week John said...

**TRH    Topic Reflection Here and Now:** Question or paraphrase of something said within the group immediately after the speaker has made the statement.

> Example:    I heard you say this job is difficult.

**TRT    Topic Reflection There and Then:** Question or paraphrase of something said within the group some time after the speaker made the point.

> Example:    Yesterday, I heard you say that the job is difficult.

\*Main Categories

Abstracted from

# A STUDY OF THE LOGIC OF TEACHING*

B. Othanel Smith
Milton O. Meux

In collaboration with
Jerrold Coombs
Daniel Eierdam
Ronald Szoke

19

*Published by Bureau of Educational Research, College of Education, University of Illinois, Urbana, Illinois, 1962.

This research was performed pursuant to a contract with the United States Office of Education, Department of Health, Education, and Welfare, Project No. 258 (7257).

# SMITH SYSTEM (Logic) SUMMARY

### SYSTEM DIMENSION

| * | ** | |
|---|-----|---|
|   | 19 | Affective |
| X | 16 | Cognitive |
|   | 6 | Work process (control) |
|   | 4 | Behavior |

### TYPE OF COMMUNICATION RECORDED

| | | |
|---|-----|---|
| X | 25 | Verbal |
|   | 7 | Nonverbal |

### SUBJECT OF OBSERVATION

| | | |
|---|-----|---|
|   | 5 | Teacher only |
|   | 2 | Student only |
| X | 19 | Teacher and student |

### DATA COLLECTION METHODS REPORTED

| | | |
|---|-----|---|
|   | 18 | Live |
|   | 13 | Tape recording without tapescript |
| X | 9 | Tape recording and tapescript |
|   | 13 | Video tape |
|   | 1 | Handwritten notes |

### AUDIO OR VIDEO TAPE REQUIRED

| | | |
|---|-----|---|
| X | 9 | Yes |
|   | 17 | No |

### PERSONNEL NEEDED FOR OBSERVATION OR RECORDING SESSION

| | | |
|---|-----|---|
|   | 17 | 1 coder |
|   | 1 | Team of 2 |
|   | 1 | 2 teams of 2 |
| X | 9 | Tape operator |

### NUMBER OF CODERS NEEDED DURING CODING SESSION

| | | |
|---|-----|---|
|   | 17 | No coder other than observer(s) |
|   | 3 | 1 coder |
|   | 2 | 2 coders |
| X | 4 | 2 teams of 2 coders |

### CODING UNITS

| | | |
|---|-----|---|
|   | 18 | Category change |
|   | 9 | Category + time unit |
| X | 6 | Content area change |
|   | 3 | Speaker change |
|   | 3 | Time sample |

### USES REPORTED BY AUTHOR

| | | |
|---|-----|---|
| X | 26 | Research |
|   | 12 | Teacher training |
|   | 9 | Supervision |

* Summary of information for this system

** Summary of information for 26 systems

19

# THE LOGIC OF TEACHING

The development of this system represents a relatively long term effort to determine a logical structure for teaching subject matter, from which an attempt was made to catalog teaching strategies.

This is a complex system requiring that tape recordings be made of the teacher-pupil interaction for later coding by two teams of two people each. The categories focus on the analysis of how teacher and pupils process content. It is expected that research with the system will determine that certain categories of behavior are more effective in teaching subject matter at different stages of the presentation of the content than are others, for example, times when it is appropriate for the teacher to use defining or describing behaviors, and others, when it is appropriate to use evaluation, opinion, or inferences.

The coding units in the Logic of Teaching system are:

1) Episodes, defined as one or more exchanges which comprise a completed verbal transaction between two or more speakers. A new episode is determined by a shift in what the speakers are talking about, which may be a new aspect, or part of a topic, or a complete change in topic.

2) Monologues, defined as a solo performance of a speaker addressing a group. Both are coded but only episodes are analyzed in this system.

## OBSERVER RELIABILITY PROCEDURES

Observer reliability procedures use two teams of two people. Each team arrives at mutual judgement of the episodes. Team judgements are used to calculate coefficient of "inter-judge agreement" for each team by dividing the number of markings agreed upon by two judges by the total number of markings of the team having the larger number of markings.

The range of reliability scores reported by the author is .62 to .73.

## SUPPLEMENTARY MATERIALS

Smith, B. O., and Meux, M. O. A Study of the Logic of Teaching. Bureau of Educational Research, College of Education, Urbana: University of Illinois, 1962.

# CATEGORIES FOR
# THE LOGIC OF TEACHING

B. O. Smith and
M.O. Meux

1. Defining

2. Describing

3. Designating

4. Stating

5. Reporting

6. Substituting

7. Evaluating

8. Opining

9. Classifying

10. Comparing and
Contrasting

11. Conditional
Inferring

12. Explaining
12.1 Mechanical
12.2 Causal
12.3 Sequent
12.4 Procedural
12.5 Teleological
12.6 Normative

13. Directing and
Managing Classroom

Abstracted from

# A STUDY OF THE STRATEGIES OF TEACHING*

**B. Othanel Smith**
**Milton Meux**
**Jerrold Coombs**
**Graham Nuthall**
**Robert Precians**

**20**

*Published by Bureau of Educational Research, College of Education, University of Illinois, Urbana, Illinois, 1967.

The research reported herein was performed pursuant to a contract with the United States Office of Education, Department of Health, Education, and Welfare. Project Number 1640.

## SMITH SYSTEM (Strategies) SUMMARY

|  | * | ** | SYSTEM DIMENSION |
|---|---|---|---|
|  |  | 19 | Affective |
|  | X | 16 | Cognitive |
|  |  | 6 | Work process (control) |
|  |  | 4 | Behavior |

### TYPE OF COMMUNICATION RECORDED

| | | |
|---|---|---|
| X | 25 | Verbal |
|  | 7 | Nonverbal |

### SUBJECT OF OBSERVATION

| | | |
|---|---|---|
|  | 5 | Teacher only |
|  | 2 | Student only |
| X | 19 | Teacher and student |

### DATA COLLECTION METHODS REPORTED

| | | |
|---|---|---|
|  | 18 | Live |
|  | 13 | Tape recording without tapescript |
| X | 9 | Tape recording and tapescript |
|  | 13 | Video tape |
|  | 1 | Handwritten notes |

### AUDIO OR VIDEO TAPE REQUIRED

| | | |
|---|---|---|
| X | 9 | Yes |
|  | 17 | No |

### PERSONNEL NEEDED FOR OBSERVATION OR RECORDING SESSION

| | | |
|---|---|---|
|  | 17 | 1 coder |
|  | 1 | Team of 2 |
|  | 1 | 2 teams of 2 |
| X | 9 | Tape operator |

### NUMBER OF CODERS NEEDED DURING CODING SESSION

| | | |
|---|---|---|
|  | 17 | No coder other than observer(s) |
|  | 3 | 1 coder |
|  | 2 | 2 coders |
| X | 4 | 2 teams of 2 coders |

### CODING UNITS

| | | |
|---|---|---|
|  | 18 | Category change |
|  | 9 | Category + time unit |
| X | 6 | Content area change |
|  | 3 | Speaker change |
|  | 3 | Time sample |

### USES REPORTED BY AUTHOR

| | | |
|---|---|---|
| X | 26 | Research |
|  | 12 | Teacher training |
|  | 9 | Supervision |

\* Summary of information for this system

\*\* Summary of information for 26 systems

# THE STRATEGIES OF TEACHING

This system is an extension of the "Logic of Teaching" study. The present system focuses on larger maneuvers having to do with control of subject matter. These maneuvers are referred to as strategies. Strategies are concerned with attaining certain outcomes and are, hence, directly related to objectives.

There are two sets of coding units:

1. Venture: which may be between two or more persons or may contain the discourse of only one speaker. A new venture is determined by a complete change in topic. The venture is more inclusive than is the episode which is the coding unit of the "Logic of Teaching" system.

2. Move: which is the logical relationships established between some event, object, thing, and some term in the proposition disclosed by the venture in which the discourse occurs. Moves are classified into major groups.

The eventual output of the study of the strategies of teaching will be the determination of appropriate strategies for teaching different stages of content development.

## OBSERVER RELIABILITY PROCEDURES

Coders are divided into two teams of two. Each team arrives at mutual judgment of the ventures. Team judgments are used to calculate the coefficient of "interjudge agreement" for each team by dividing the number of markings agreed upon by the two judges by the total number of markings for the team having the larger number of markings. The range of reliability scores reported is .56 to .89.

## SUPPLEMENTARY MATERIALS

Smith, B. O., et al. A Study of the Strategies of Teaching. Bureau of Educational Research, College of Education, Urbana: University of Illinois, April, 1967.

# CATEGORIES FOR

## STRATEGIES OF TEACHING

B. O. Smith, M. O. Meux, J. Coombs, G. Nuthall, R. Precians

## INSTRUCTIONS FOR CLASSIFYING VENTURES

1. Each venture can be classified by its cognitive objective into one of the following categories: causal, conceptual, evaluative, informatory, interpretive, procedural, reason, rule, and system ventures.

2. Read the entire venture for the sense of it as a whole. Then read it again and try to formulate the question with which the venture deals. For example, does it deal with the cause of something? Does it attempt to get at the reasons for an act, decision, or whatnot? Is it merely informative? By using the criteria given for each category, classify the venture into the category which it fits best.

3. No venture may have more than one objective.

4. If a venture is very difficult to classify, put it aside. When the easier cases have been grouped, return to the more difficult ones.

5. In some cases it is difficult to tell whether a venture belongs in the reason or in the rule category. Where there are a number of specific decisions or actions falling in a particular category and all regulated by the same rule or justified by the same reason (e.g., students are asked to decide which words in a number of sentences are verbs), the venture is to be called a rule venture. If the specific decision or action is justifiable by different reasons (e.g., students are asked why Mr. X went into the house), the venture is to be classified as a reason venture.

6. It is sometimes difficult to decide whether or not to put a venture in the evaluative category, although it contains a number of value judgments about different objects, ideas, etc. As a rule, when a venture centers in the evaluation of a single object, event, and the like, it is to be classed in the evaluative category. If the venture contains a number of evaluations about a number of different objects, events, reasons, and so forth, along with other materials, it does not belong among the evaluative ventures.

7. Information ventures are sometimes difficult to distinguish from other sorts of ventures because almost all ventures are informative. However, when information is given concerning the classificatory characteristics of an object or entity, and when information is given in response to some dominant logical enterprise such as evaluation, explanation, etc., the venture should not be classified as an informatory venture.

# CRITERIA FOR CLASSIFYING VENTURES

1. <u>Causal Venture</u>. The primary cognitive import of this kind of venture is the identification, description, or discussion of events, agents, or characteristics of events or agents which are said to cause, generate, or facilitate the occurrence of a particular phenomenon or class of phenomena. A causal venture is identified as one which satisfies one, or more than one, of the following criteria:

    1.1 A phenomenon is mentioned or discussed and the class engages in a discussion of the events, changes, agents, forces, or conditions which originate, lead to, or facilitate the phenomenon's occurrence.

    1.2 A phenomenon is mentioned or discussed and the class engages in a discussion of the dispositions or qualities of an agent or object that relates the phenomenon to some general law.

    1.3 A phenomenon, circumstance, or outcome is mentioned or discussed and the class discusses one or more means by which the phenomenon, circumstance, or outcome may be brought about.

2. <u>Conceptual Venture</u>. The primary cognitive import of this type of venture is that of disclosing the conditions or criteria governing the use of a term. A term may be a single word such as 'imperialism,' and expression of two or more words such as 'coefficient of expansion,' or a proper name such as 'Andrew Jackson.' A conceptual venture may be identified by one or more of the following criteria:

    2.1 An X is mentioned and the class discussion is primarily directed to such questions as: What is X? What does X mean? What do we mean by X? How can we tell when something is an X?

    2.2 Something is named or referred to, and the class discussion is mainly devoted to describing its characteristics, functions, uses, or parts.

    2.3 Something is named or referred to, and the class discussion is primarily devoted to mentioning or considering examples of it.

3. <u>Evaluative Venture</u>. The primary cognitive import of this sort of venture is to decide whether X is good or bad, right or wrong, fair or unfair, and the like. An evaluative venture may be identified by one or more of the following criteria:

    3.1 One or more characteristics, actions, policies, and the like are given and the class tries to decide the value category in which they belong, although no decision may be reached.

    3.2 One or more value categories are given and the students try to name or describe objects, events, characteristics, actions, and the like, that belong in the categories.

    3.3 A particular case of human conduct or line of reasoning is examined and the class tries to decide the value category to which it belongs, although no decision may be reached.

4.  Informatory Venture. The primary cognitive import of the informatory venture is the provision of information or evidence to clarify or amplify a specified topic or group of related topics. The central concern of the discussion in this type of venture is the answering of questions such as, "What happened?" "When did it happen?" "What did it do?" "Who or what did it?" or "What is it like?" This type of venture may be identified by one or more of the following criteria:

4.1  One or more objects, events, or actions are mentioned or suggested and the class gives a description of it.

4.2  Some historical event or development is mentioned or alluded to and the class discusses the events and actions surrounding or comprising it.

4.3  A particular topic or event is mentioned or suggested and the class gives instances of a specified set of functional or descriptive characteristics, e.g., "What are the industries of Canada?" "What are the costs of crime?" 'Canada' and 'crime' are the topics, and 'industries' and 'costs' are the sets of characteristics for which instances are given.

4.4  Two or more objects or events are mentioned or suggested and the class describes each one by way of comparing them.

4.5  Exercises such as compositions are presented to the class either by students or teachers as examples.

5.  Interpretive Venture. The primary cognitive import of this sort of venture is that of disclosing the meaning or significance of a set of words or symbols or a bit of discourse. Usually, the set of words or bit of discourse with which a venture is concerned is taken from a literary work. An interpretive venture is identified by one or more of the following criteria:

5.1  A set of words or bit of discourse previously written or spoken is either given or explicitly referred to, and the class attempts to translate the meaning of the set of words or passage into a different set of words.

5.2  A set of words or bit of discourse previously written or spoken and constituting a metaphor or an allegory is either given or explicitly referred to, and the class attempts to state the literal meaning of the words or passage.

5.3  A set of words or bit of discourse previously written or spoken is either given or explicitly referred to, and the class attempts to draw inferences or conclusions about persons, objects, or events mentioned or described by the set of words or the passage.

5.4  An expression, object, event, or character is mentioned and the class or teacher deals with the question of what it symbolizes.

6.  Procedural Venture. The primary cognitive import of the procedural venture is a step-by-step description of how to perform an activity, reach a solution, carry through a plan, or the like. The procedural venture may be identified by the following criteria:

6.1  The class or teacher analyzes a course of action, as in a recipe or in the instructions for carrying on an experiment, into steps or phases designed to reach a particular end.

6 - Smith, et al.

6.2 The class or teacher analyzes a symbolic process, as in an algebraic solution or the symbolic representation of a chemical reaction, into steps or phases.

6.3 The class or teacher represents symbolically a chemical reaction or physical process so as to indicate, at least in a very general way, a procedure for, or considerations required in, making such representation.

7. <u>Reason Venture</u>. The primary cognitive import of this sort of venture is the identification or discussion of the reasons for an action, event, or conclusion. A reason is taken to mean the considerations or conditions given to justify a particular action, event, or conclusion. A venture of this type is identified as one for which one, or more, of the following criteria hold:

7.1 A person's action or course of action is given, and the class discusses the desires, purposes, or beliefs used to justify it.

7.2 A course of action or particular act is given, and the functions, ends, or outcomes used to justify or account for the adoption or execution of the action (or which account for the failure to adopt or execute the action) are discussed.

7.3 A judgment or conclusion is given and the evidence needed to justify or defend it is discussed.

7.4 An action, course of action, or state of affairs is given and the legal regulations or regulatory rules used to justify or account for it (or which account for the action or state of affairs not occurring) are discussed.

8. <u>Rule Venture</u>. The primary cognitive import of this kind of venture is either the making of decisions based on rules or identification and use of rules in the performance of an exercise or activity. A rule is a conventional guide or regulation for action, as in the rules of grammar or mathematics. A rule venture is identified by one or more of the following criteria:

8.1 The discourse gives one or more cases involving one or more rules and the class is asked to make decisions as to what is the correct way of dealing with the case or cases. After a number of cases have been dealt with, the rule is usually stated by either the student or the teacher.

8.2 The rule or rules are explicitly given in the discourse and the student is asked to apply them to one or more cases.

8.3 A rule or formula which is used or intended for use in solving problems is discussed with respect to its derivation or logical or mathematical basis.

9. <u>System Venture</u>. The primary cognitive import of this type of venture is that of disclosing the functional interrelationships of the parts of some unit that operates to produce or secure a given end. A paradigm case of a system is the electrical circuit in a radio. Each part plays a role in the over-all function of the radio which is to receive radio waves and translate them into sounds. A system venture is to be identified by one or more of the following criteria:

9.1 The discussion as a whole attempts to answer the question, "How does X work?"

9.2 The discussion as a whole describes the way a number of objects, events, or actions work together to fulfill a certain function.

# DEFINITIONS

## LEVEL I

Retrieving

Deliberate recovering or regaining by remembering, recalling and reflecting.

Reflecting

Thinking back over, reminiscing, contemplating, mulling over.

Remembering

Having a notion or idea come into the mind again which implies an earlier experience; random or passive memory.

Recalling

Deliberate bringing back to mind, recollecting; purposeful or active memory.

Indentifying

Labeling, recognizing by discriminating; simple agreement or disagreement with another's statement.

Discriminating

Detecting, distinguishing by certain features or characteristics, discerning.

Perceiving

Being openly and selectively aware.

Sensing

Obtaining information through the senses.

## LEVEL II

Inferring

Assuming cause and effect or associational relationships among facts; assigning meaning that is beyond the data.

Comparing and Contrasting

Examining things in terms of their characteristics; things are compared when they set side by side in order to show their likenesses.  They are also set side by side in order to emphasize their differences.

Imagining

Responding to properties of an object or event not present to the senses; the mental synthesis of ideas from elements experienced separately.

Exploring

Deliberate wondering about, searching into, questioning about; penetrating into a field, area or condition.

Organizing

Arranging or systematizing the interdependent parts of a whole, elaborating a point or supporting an argument; relating.

## Analyzing

Examining something to distinguish its component parts separately, or in relation to the whole.

## LEVEL III

## Defining

Drawing together and stating the essential qualities of a concept or thing and identifying its precise significance. The most precise definitions are equivalence relationships obeying the "if and only if" test. (Defining as used here does not include mere repetition of a definition arrived at earlier.)

## Judging

Drawing a conclusion or making a decision through a deliberate rational process. (If the answer yes or no is given and a reason for the answer is given, the mental process is discriminate.)

## Evaluating

Rating something by accepted criteria or by the personal values or biases which are made known.

## Discovering

Identifying for the first time something not previously perceived by the discoverer; oftentimes this is spontaneous.

## Hypothesizing

Provisionally accepting a proposition, condition, or principle in order to draw out its logical consequence in accordance with facts which are known or which may be determined; predicting.

## Abstracting

Lifting out one or more qualities or factors to achieve a new relationship or different conceptualization.

## Integrating

Assimilating and/or accommodating. In assimilating, the factors seem to fit immediately and without rearrangement or adjustment. In accommodation, the data furnished by the experience are seen as discrepant; they do not fit with one's present notions or patterns of thought, therefore some rearrangement, readjustment or re-formulation is required in order to match perceived events.

## LEVEL IV

## Creating

Inventing, generalizing, synthesizing with considerable personal involvement and with results that become recognized by others as having value. (This definition does not include the use of creative as an adjective.)

## Generalizing

Stating relationships, principles, laws covering all cases in a class. (This definition does not include mere repetition of a generalization arrived at earlier.)

## Inventing-Composing

Bringing together elements, factors, objects, in some new form or use.

## Synthesizing

Conceptualizing which brings elements, ideas or generalizations together which have not been brought together in this manner before.

Abstracted from

# AN INTRODUCTION TO THE USE OF THE COPING ANALYSIS SCHEDULE FOR EDUCATIONAL SETTINGS (CASES)

and

# THE SPAULDING TEACHER ACTIVITY RATING SCHEDULE (STARS)*

Robert L. Spaulding

21
22

*Published by Education Improvement Program, Duke University, Durham, North Carolina, 1967.

# COPING ANALYSIS SCHEDULE FOR EDUCATIONAL SETTING (CASES) SUMMARY

### SYSTEM DIMENSION

| * | ** | |
|---|---|---|
| X | 19 | Affective |
| | 16 | Cognitive |
| | 6 | Work process (control) |
| X | 4 | Behavior |

### TYPE OF COMMUNICATION RECORDED

| | | |
|---|---|---|
| X | 25 | Verbal |
| X | 7 | Nonverbal |

### SUBJECT OF OBSERVATION

| | | |
|---|---|---|
| | 5 | Teacher only |
| X | 2 | Student only |
| | 19 | Teacher and student |

### DATA COLLECTION METHODS REPORTED

| | | |
|---|---|---|
| X | 18 | Live |
| | 13 | Tape recording without tapescript |
| | 9 | Tape recording and tapescript |
| | 13 | Video tape |
| | 1 | Handwritten notes |

### AUDIO OR VIDEO TAPE REQUIRED

| | | |
|---|---|---|
| | 9 | Yes |
| X | 17 | No |

### PERSONNEL NEEDED FOR OBSERVATION OR RECORDING SESSION

| | | |
|---|---|---|
| X | 17 | 1 coder |
| | 1 | Team of 2 |
| | 1 | 2 teams of 2 |
| | 9 | Tape operator |

### NUMBER OF CODERS NEEDED DURING CODING SESSION

| | | |
|---|---|---|
| X | 17 | No coder other than observer(s) |
| | 3 | 1 coder |
| | 2 | 2 coders |
| | 4 | 2 teams of 2 coders |

### CODING UNITS

| | | |
|---|---|---|
| | 18 | Category change |
| | 9 | Category + time unit |
| | 6 | Content area change |
| | 3 | Speaker change |
| X | 3 | Time sample |

### USES REPORTED BY AUTHOR

| | | |
|---|---|---|
| X | 26 | Research |
| X | 12 | Teacher training |
| X | 9 | Supervision |

* Summary of information for this system

** Summary of information for 26 systems

# SPAULDING TEACHER ACTIVITY
# RATING SCHEDULE ·(STARS) SUMMARY

|   *   |  **  | SYSTEM DIMENSION |
|-------|------|------------------|
| X | 19 | Affective |
| X | 16 | Cognitive |
| X | 6 | Work process (control) |
| X | 4 | Behavior |

### TYPE OF COMMUNICATION RECORDED

| | | |
|---|---|---|
| X | 25 | Verbal |
| X | 7 | Nonverbal |

### SUBJECT OF OBSERVATION

| | | |
|---|---|---|
| X | 5 | Teacher only |
| | 2 | Student only |
| | 19 | Teacher and student |

### DATA COLLECTION METHODS REPORTED

| | | |
|---|---|---|
| X | 18 | Live |
| | 13 | Tape recording without tapescript |
| | 9 | Tape recording and tapescript |
| | 13 | Video tape |
| | 1 | Handwritten notes |

### AUDIO OR VIDEO TAPE REQUIRED

| | | |
|---|---|---|
| | 9 | Yes |
| X | 17 | No |

### PERSONNEL NEEDED FOR OBSERVATION OR RECORDING SESSION

| | | |
|---|---|---|
| X | 17 | 1 coder |
| | 1 | Team of 2 |
| | 1 | 2 teams of 2 |
| | 9 | Tape operator |

### NUMBER OF CODERS NEEDED DURING CODING SESSION

| | | |
|---|---|---|
| X | 17 | No coder other than observer(s) |
| | 3 | 1 coder |
| | 2 | 2 coders |
| | 4 | 2 teams of 2 coders |

### CODING UNITS

| | | |
|---|---|---|
| | 18 | Category change |
| | 9 | Category + time unit |
| | 6 | Content area change |
| | 3 | Speaker change |
| X | 3 | Time sample |

### USES REPORTED BY AUTHOR

| | | |
|---|---|---|
| X | 26 | Research |
| X | 12 | Teacher training |
| X | 9 | Supervision |

* Summary of information for this system

** Summary of information for 26 systems

# COPING ANALYSIS SCHEDULE FOR EDUCATIONAL SETTING (CASES)
## and
# THE SPAULDING TEACHER ACTIVITY RATING SCHEDULE (STARS)

Both of these systems are affective; and although they use transactional cues to code the data, STARS codes teacher behavior alone, and CASES student behavior.

Both of these systems can be used "live" by observers in the classroom. These systems are unique in their emphasis on motor and nonverbal behaviors of the pupils, and thus the CASES system can provide useful information about children as young as two years of age and STARS about how teachers work with these young children.

The systems have been used for a variety of purposes including the selection of children for behavior modification programs.

STARS provides a measure for determining the teacher's approach to control in the classroom by the use of such categories as "setting performance goals" and "prescribing" certain kinds of activities. STARS and CASES can be used to give feedback to teachers and, presumably, parents about their interaction with the very young pupil and about pupils' reactions to varying instructional styles.

Observers coding in this system use a time sampling technique, with a time period ranging from 3 to 10 seconds.

## OBSERVER RELIABILITY PROCEDURES

CASES: Reliability of observation and coding is obtained by simultaneous observations of representative types of children during several 30- or 40-minute periods. The reported range of reliability scores is .78 to .96.

STARS: Reliability of observation and coding is obtained by simultaneous observations of teachers during several 30- or 40-minute periods.

Reliability for separate parts of the instrument range from .75 to .95.

## SUPPLEMENTARY MATERIALS
### CASES

Computer programs for the processing of data from CASES for an IBM System 360 Model 75 are available from the Durham Educational Improvement Program.

Spaulding, R. L. An Introduction to the Use of the Coping Analysis Schedule for Educational Settings (CASES). Durham, N. Carolina: Education Improvement Program, Duke University, 1967

Spaulding, R. L. Special Studies using CASES. Durham, N. Carolina: Durham Education Improvement Program, Duke University.

STARS

Computer programs for·the processing of data from STARS for an IBM System 360 Model 75 are available from the Durham Education Improvement Program.

Spaulding, R. L. The Spaulding Teacher Rating Schedule (STARS). Durham, N. Carolina: Education Improvement Program, Duke University, 1967

Spaulding, R. L. Special Studies using STARS. Durham, N. Carolina: Durham Education Improvement Program, Duke University.

CATEGORIES FOR

A COPING ANALYSIS SCHEDULE
FOR EDUCATIONAL SETTINGS (CASES)*

R. L. Spaulding

1. Aggressive Behavior:
   Direct attack: grabbing, pushing, hitting, pulling, kicking, name-calling; Destroying property: smashing, tearing, breaking.

2. Negative (Inappropriate) Attention-Getting Behavior:
   Annoying, bothering, whining, loud talking (unnecessarily), attention getting aversive noise-making, belittling, criticizing.

3. Manipulating and Directing Others:
   Manipulating, bossing, commanding, directing, enforcing rules, conniving, wheedling, controlling.

4. Resisting Authority:
   Resisting, delaying; passive aggressive behavior; pretending to conform, conforming to the letter but not the spirit; defensive checking.

5. Self-Directed Activity:
   Productive working; reading, writing, constructing with interest; self-directed dramatic play (with high involvement).

6. Paying Rapt Attention:
   Listening attentively, watching carefully; concentrating on a story being told, a film being watched, a record played.

7. Sharing and Helping:
   Contributing ideas, interests, materials, helping; responding by showing feelings (laughing, smiling, etc.) in audience situations; initiating conversation.

8. Social Interaction:
   Mutual give and take, cooperative behavior, integrative social behavior; studying or working together where participants are on a par.

9. Seeking Support, Assistance and Information:
   Bidding or asking teachers or significant peers for help, support, sympathy, affection, etc., being helped; receiving assistance.

10. Following directions passively and submissively:
    Doing assigned work without enthusiasm or great interest; submitting to requests; answering directed questions; waiting for instructions as directed.

11. Observing Passively:
    Visual wandering; watching others work; checking on noises or movements; checking on activities of adults or peers.

12. Responding to Internal Stimuli:
    Daydreaming; sleeping; rocking or fidgeting; (not in transaction with external stimuli).

13. Physical Withdrawal or Avoidance:
    Flight; moving away; hiding: avoiding transactions by movement away or around.

Note: Categories 5 through 10 are further coded as a or b in structured settings to indicate appropriate or inappropriate behavior (based on social expectations for the setting). Example: 5a would be recorded when a child was painting during art period (when painting was one of the expected activities). Painting during "story time" or an academic setting would normally be coded 5b.

* © 1966 Robert L. Spaulding, Education Improvement Program, Duke University.

# CATEGORIES FOR

## THE SPAULDING TEACHER ACTIVITY RATING SCHEDULE (STARS)*

### R. L. Spaulding

A. Molar Categories:

Cognitive Structuring - Teacher-child transactions focusing on modification of thinking and conceptual structures.

Behavior Management - Teacher-child transactions focusing on modification of social transactions, impulse control, and classroom routine.

Motor Structuring - Teacher-child transactions focusing on modification of motor activities, including fine and gross motor control.

Converse - Teacher-child transactions not focused on modification of child behavior. Coded as Talk or List depending on direction of transaction.

Non-child - Teacher behaviors not child transactional. Coded as Adult (for teacher-other adult transactions) and Pers (for personal activities).

B. Modification Categories:

Appr - Teacher operants with generally reinforcing affect

Disapp - Teacher operants with generally punishing affect (aversive)

Do - Teacher operants setting or eliciting performance goals and action

Don't - Teacher operants proscribing certain actions (without aversive affect)

Neu - Teacher operants conveying information (but not setting or eliciting performance)

List - Teacher attending to child or group operants

_____

* © 1967 Robert L. Spaulding, Education Improvement Program, Duke University.

Abstracted from

# NINE COLLECTED WORKS*

William R. Crawford
Shu-Kie Ho
Anthony H. McNaughton
Hilda Taba
Norman E. Wallen

*Unpublished documents from the Taba Curriculum Development Project, San Francisco State College, San Francisco, California.

This research was performed pursuant to a contract with the United States Department of Health, Education and Welfare, Office of Education, under the provisions of the Cooperative Research Program.

# TABA SYSTEM SUMMARY

### SYSTEM DIMENSION

| * | ** | |
|---|---|---|
| X | 19 | Affective |
| X | 16 | Cognitive |
| | 6 | Work process (control) |
| | 4 | Behavior |

### TYPE OF COMMUNICATION RECORDED

| | | |
|---|---|---|
| X | 25 | Verbal |
| | 7 | Nonverbal |

### SUBJECT OF OBSERVATION

| | | |
|---|---|---|
| | 5 | Teacher only |
| | 2 | Student only |
| X | 19 | Teacher and student |

### DATA COLLECTION METHODS REPORTED

| | | |
|---|---|---|
| | 18 | Live |
| | 13 | Tape recording without tapescript |
| X | 9 | Tape recording and tapescript |
| | 13 | Video tape |
| | 1 | Handwritten notes |

### AUDIO OR VIDEO TAPE REQUIRED

| | | |
|---|---|---|
| X | 9 | Yes |
| | 17 | No |

### PERSONNEL NEEDED FOR OBSERVATION OR RECORDING SESSION

| | | |
|---|---|---|
| | 17 | 1 coder |
| | 1 | Team of 2 |
| | 1 | 2 teams of 2 |
| X | 9 | Tape operator |

### NUMBER OF CODERS NEEDED DURING CODING SESSION

| | | |
|---|---|---|
| | 17 | No coder other than observer(s) |
| X | 3 | 1 coder |
| | 2 | 2 coders |
| | 4 | 2 teams of 2 coders |

### CODING UNITS

| | | |
|---|---|---|
| | 18 | Category change |
| | 9 | Category + time unit |
| X | 6 | Content area change |
| | 3 | Speaker change |
| | 3 | Time sample |

### USES REPORTED BY AUTHOR

| | | |
|---|---|---|
| X | 26 | Research |
| X | 12 | Teacher training |
| | 9 | Supervision |

* Summary of information for this system

** Summary of information for 26 systems

23

# THE TABA SYSTEM

This system is part of a curriculum development project and represents Taba's hypothesis that the content and the approach to the content are inseparable. She developed teaching strategies for teaching social studies grades 1 through 6 which are reflected in the category system. The strategies are based on the concept that pupils' learning of attitudes, values, and skills such as learning how to learn, cannot be treated as independent of the content that the child is learning. Thus, the strategies help the teacher take a class through certain well defined steps in learning new material.

The child learns, for instance, to operate on a data level; that is, to collect data, to group these data, and to label these groups (give them names), learns the procedures for grouping elements into category systems, learns to make his criteria for grouping explicit, and learns that there are multiple classifications for any set of data. The child learns how to make inferences from data, or from groupings or from categories, to make predictions, to make inferences from data and to make logical inference and learns to generalize from the inferences. These learnings occur through the use of teacher strategies which are made operational through prescription of certain categories at certain stages of teaching content.

The system contains categories which can help a teacher learn if he is operating on the appropriate thought level such as "extension of thought unit to a lower level," "extension of thought unit to the same or higher level" and "reiteration of an idea at the same thought level."

Taba's efforts are unique in that she focused on increasing the participation of all students in her class so that the entire class operates on the appropriate level of thought at any particular time. Her strategies mitigate against having "brighter" pupils operate on an abstract level while the "slower" pupils operate on a concrete level. She feels that the "jumpers," as she describes them, need the data that data-oriented students can provide in order to make valid generations and inferences. Her strategies focus on bringing a whole class along together from one level of abstraction to the next.

One study by Taba indicated that when taught by teachers trained to use the strategies, children of lower I.Q.'s operate as easily on higher levels of thought as do pupils of higher I.Q.'s. Thus, these strategies seem to allow for more effective learning for all the children and are an approach to group learning likely to gain considerable attention.

Taba's work is also unique in that she built in strategies for working with pupil attitudes and values simultaneously with learning social studies content. Although the system was developed for use in social studies classes, it seems to be applicable to other subject matter areas.

The unit of coding for this system is a remark or series of remarks expressing a complete idea, serving a specified function, and classifiable according to a level of thought.

## OBSERVER RELIABILITY PROCEDURE

No range of reliability scores reported.

## SUPPLEMENTARY MATERIALS

Taba, Hilda. Thinking in Elementary School Children. San Francisco: San Francisco State College, 1964.

The following nine works are unpublished documents by members of the Curriculum Development Project, San Francisco State College, San Francisco, California:

1. "Coding Scheme," H. Taba
2. "The Use of Teaching Modules to Study High Level Thinking in the Social Studies," A. H. McNaughton, N. E. Wallen, S. Ho, and W. R. Crawford.
3. "Informal Evaluation of Listing, Categorizing and Labeling Skills," A. H. McNaughton.
4. "Test Exercises in Listing, Grouping, Labeling and Generalizing Skills," A. H. McNaughton.
5. "Informal Tests on Concepts and Generalizations," A. H. McNaughton.
6. "Informal Evaluation of the Ability to Interpret Data in Written Materials and Make Inferences from Them," A. H. McNaughton.
7. "Measuring Cognitive Elements in Attitudes," A. H. McNaughton.
8. "A Generalization is a Generalization," A. H. McNaughton.
9. "One Model for Disseminating Curriculum Innovations: Problems, Processes and Possibilities," H. Taba.

# CATEGORIES FOR

# THE TABA SYSTEM

## H. Taba, et. al

## Source

| | | |
|---|---|---|
| TG | Teacher Gives |
| TS | Teacher Seeks |
| CG | Child Gives |
| CS | Child Seeks |

## Thought Levels (Any of these can take functions)

0      Incorrect information
1      Specific items of data
2      Relating, comparing, contrasting items of data
     2.1    Grouping
     2.2    Labeling
     2.3    Recognizing multiple classification
3      Factual explanation, or factual support of prediction
4      Inference from units of data or from groupings and categorization; predictions
5      Inferential explanation, inferential (logical) support of prediction
6      Generalization from inferences

## Functions

*A      Agreement or approval
C1      Clarification
*CM      Classroom management - discipline (teacher only)
*D      Disagreement or disapproval
*DM      Discussion management
*Ir      Irrelevant
R      Reiteration of immediately preceding thought unit
R+      Reiteration of thought unit given earlier in the discussion
Sp      Extension of thought unit directed toward more specificity at the same or lower level; "Give me an example."
Sum      Teacher summarizes more than one thought unit
X      Extension of thought unit at same or higher level

* Do not take thought levels

This material is not to be reproduced in any form. It is being produced under a Cooperative Research Project (OE6-10-182) supported by the U. S. Office of Education under the provision of Public Law 531.

# CODING SCHEME

## The Unit of Coding

A "thought unit" is defined as a remark, or series of remarks, which expresses a more or less complete idea, and serves a specified function. It is therefore possible for a single word, a part of a sentence, a sentence, or an entire paragraph, to be designated as a thought unit. The end of a thought unit is indicated by a slash. For example,

| | |
|---|---|
| Girl | Another thing...well, education helps us/ because well, if...like, if a one-product country goes/ well, it just is not good anymore/ then well, if you didn't have education,/ you could not communicate with other countries./ |
| T | Is it important to communicate?/ |

* * *

| | |
|---|---|
| Boy | ...so he has to pay for the gas himself/ and if he raises the price/ then nobody's going to come along and buy his gas./ |
| T | So this is what Johnson says that prices seem to be heading to a degree of... all right, say it some more, Bruce./ |

## Identification of Speaker

This code describes the source of the thought unit (the teacher or a student), and whether the speaker is giving or seeking information. The code symbols are:

CG   -   Child Gives.

| Harold: | You can't buy firecrackers here. | CG |
|---|---|---|

CS   -   Child Seeks.

| Joan: | Where can you buy them? | CS |
|---|---|---|

TG   -   Teacher Gives.

| T: | It's against the law to sell them. | TG |
|---|---|---|

TS   -   Teacher Seeks.

| T: | Where do we see lots of firecrackers? | TS |
|---|---|---|

## Thought Level Codes

O   -   Incorrect information in thought unit

| Peter: | They found the Northwest passage in California | CG O |
|---|---|---|

1   -   Correct enumeration, giving units of data

| | | CG 1 |
|---|---|---|
| John: | The lady was trying to cure by the egg. | CG 1 |

6 - Taba, et al.

| | | |
|---|---|---|
| Carol: | Sometimes the wagons got stuck in the snow and people got killed. | CG 1 |

2    -   Relating, comparing, contrasting units of data

| | | |
|---|---|---|
| Mary: | In the West Indies they speak French, and in Brazil they speak Portuguese, and in the rest of the countries they speak Spanish. | CG 2 |

---

| | | |
|---|---|---|
| John: | Well, the pioneers weren't traveling on the ocean, like the colonists, they were traveling on just land. | CG 2 |

2.1   -   Grouping

| | | |
|---|---|---|
| Harry: | I think that "people" and "children" should go with "Pilgrims" and "Indians." | CG 2.1 |

---

| | | |
|---|---|---|
| Mary: | Those things are both about buildings. | CG 2.1 |

2.2   -   Labeling, (Categorizing) and Subsuming on a Single Basis

| | | |
|---|---|---|
| Eddie: | "Trains" go under "transportation." | CG 2.2 |

---

| | | |
|---|---|---|
| Tom: | "English" and "Dutch" go under "explorers." | CG 2.2 |

2.3   -   Recognition of Multiple Classification

Correct categorizing of a single item in more than one category:

| | | |
|---|---|---|
| Cathy: | "Church" can go under "architecture" and it can go under "religion" both. | CG 2.3 |

3    -   Factual explanation, or factual support of prediction

| | | |
|---|---|---|
| Patty: | (Life was harder on the missions than on the Ranchos) because on the ranchos they had experienced Indians to help them. | CG 3 |

---

| | | |
|---|---|---|
| Babs: | (The children washed at school) because they don't have time to go home after they work in the corn fields. | CG 3 |

4    -   Giving inference from units of data

| | | |
|---|---|---|
| John: | (When you're traveling right in the middle of the Atlantic Ocean), it's pretty much the same all the way along. | CG 4 |

Frances: I don't see how that wise woman could predict what                   CG 4
the baby was going to be.

5 - Providing an inferential explanation

Tom: (I'd rather have been with the colonists) because if I
was a pioneer I'd have to walk all those miles and I
don't think my feet would ever feel the same.                          CG 5

_____

Karl: (But the colonists had more security) because they were
more in bunches than the pioneers were.                                  CG 5

6 - Generalization from inferences

Harry: (Some people say that a long time ago Africa was hooked
on to South America. There's a possibility that people
moved from Africa to South America) and they just fol-
lowed their customs ever since.                                         CG 6

_____

Bob: The witch doctors are trying to do with wands and cracked
eggs what our medical doctors do with needles.                          CG 6

Functions

*A - Agreement or Approval. A thought unit that states or seeks agreement with, or
approval of, the content of a previously given thought unit.

Claire: I think so, too.                                                   CG A

T: That's a good point, Joan.                                             TG A

CL - Clarification.

Lois: Do you mean in the story?                                            CS C1

T: Yes, I mean - what happened to John?                                   TG C1

*CM - Classroom Management. These thought units are statements which the teacher uses
to establish discipline, restore order to the classroom, or to control an individual.
Its use is restricted to remarks by the teacher.

T: Put your hands down for a minute.                                       TG CM

T: We'll have to take our turns and wait for the other
person to finish.                                                        TG CM

_____

* Do not take thought levels.

8 - Taba, et al.

*D - Disagreement or Disapproval.  Such a thought unit states or seeks disagreement with, or disapproval of, the content of a previously given thought unit.

| | | |
|---|---|---|
| Carol: | I don't agree with Jane. | CG D |
| T: | That's not quite accurate, Betty. | TG D |

*DM - Discussion Management.  This code is used whenever a child or the teacher makes a statement which concerns the management of the discussion.

| | | |
|---|---|---|
| John: | Getting back to what Betty Jo said about taxes ... | CG DM |
| T: | We have quite a long list here now.  I think that's enough. | TG DM |

*IR - Irrelevancies.  Statements which are outside the focus of the discussion.

| | | |
|---|---|---|
| Jean: | (During a discussion of what is found in stores) My mother always shops at Jones' market. | CG Ir |
| T: | (During a discussion of what the class knew about California, a child remarked that it has many state parks) And you know how full they get in the summertime. | TG Ir |

R - Reiteration.  These are statements by the teacher or a child that restate what already has been said in the immediately preceding thought unit.

| | | |
|---|---|---|
| Carol: | California is a state. | CG 1 |
| T: | All right, California is a state. | TG 1 R |
| T: | What did you say? | TS R |
| John: | I said they came to California in wagons. | CG 1 R |

R+ - The sole difference between R (Reiteration) and R+ is that R+ refers to thought units other than the immediately preceding one.  Pages of dialogue may occur between the original statement and the thought unit coded R+.

Sp - Specification.  This code applies when the speaker is seeking or giving specific instances of a general statement.  It seldom appears at the higher thought levels.

| | | |
|---|---|---|
| Charles: | We'll need some things that suck up water. | CG 4 |
| T: | What do we call things that suck up water? | TS 1 Sp |
| Fred: | Pumps. | CG 1 Sp |

Sum - Teacher summarizes and reiterates more than one thought unit.

| | | |
|---|---|---|
| T: | All right, Peter says he thinks we should have stricter gun laws because too many people get killed. / Jack says people have a right to have guns/ and Joan said there should be tests ... | TG 4 Sum TG 4 Sum TG 4 Sum |

* Do not take thought levels.

X  -  <u>Extension</u>.   These are remarks (or questions intended to do so), which develop thought on the same or higher level, either for further ideas or for clarification of the preceding idea.

|  |  |  |
|---|---|---|
| (Carol: | There's a place in California called Death Valley). | CG 1 |
| John: | It's the hottest spot.  It goes up to 128$^\circ$. | CG 1X |

---

| | | |
|---|---|---|
| Fred: | Well, a lot of people would move in to get the oil, / | CG 4 |
| | and then they'd have to build some way to get water in. | CG 4X |

Abstracted from

# SOCIAL-EMOTIONAL CLIMATE INDEX*
## and
## THE DEVELOPMENT OF A TECHNIQUE FOR THE MEASUREMENT OF SOCIAL-EMOTIONAL CLIMATE IN CLASSROOMS **

John Withall

24

*Unpublished document, Pennsylvania State University, University Park, Pennsylvania, Undated, (mimeo).
**From the **Journal of Experimental Education,** 17:(3) 347-361, March, 1949

# SOCIAL-EMOTIONAL CLIMATE INDEX SUMMARY

|   | * | ** | SYSTEM DIMENSION |
|---|---|----|------------------|
|   | X | 19 | Affective |
|   | X | 16 | Cognitive |
|   |   | 6  | Work process (control) |
|   |   | 4  | Behavior |

### TYPE OF COMMUNICATION RECORDED

| * | ** | |
|---|----|--|
| X | 25 | Verbal |
|   | 7  | Nonverbal |

### SUBJECT OF OBSERVATION

| * | ** | |
|---|----|--|
| X | 5  | Teacher only |
|   | 2  | Student only |
|   | 19 | Teacher and student |

### DATA COLLECTION METHODS REPORTED

| * | ** | |
|---|----|--|
| X | 18 | Live |
| X | 13 | Tape recording without tapescript |
|   | 9  | Tape recording and tapescript |
| X | 13 | Video tape |
|   | 1  | Handwritten notes |

### AUDIO OR VIDEO TAPE REQUIRED

| * | ** | |
|---|----|--|
|   | 9  | Yes |
| X | 17 | No |

### PERSONNEL NEEDED FOR OBSERVATION OR RECORDING SESSION

| * | ** | |
|---|----|--|
| X | 17 | 1 coder |
|   | 1  | Team of 2 |
|   | 1  | 2 teams of 2 |
|   | 9  | Tape operator |

### NUMBER OF CODERS NEEDED DURING CODING SESSION

| * | ** | |
|---|----|--|
| X | 17 | No coder other than observer(s) |
|   | 3  | 1 coder |
|   | 2  | 2 coders |
|   | 4  | 2 teams of 2 coders |

### CODING UNITS

| * | ** | |
|---|----|--|
| X | 18 | Category change |
|   | 9  | Category + time unit |
|   | 6  | Content area change |
|   | 3  | Speaker change |
|   | 3  | Time sample |

### USES REPORTED BY AUTHOR

| * | ** | |
|---|----|--|
| X | 26 | Research |
| X | 12 | Teacher training |
| X | 9  | Supervision |

* Summary of information for this system

** Summary of information for 26 systems

# THE SOCIAL-EMOTIONAL CLIMATE INDEX

This system, one of the earliest of the classroom observation systems, was developed in the late 1940's at the University of Chicago. It draws very heavily on the pioneering work of H. H. Anderson, who developed a comprehensive system for assessing the effects of teacher behaviors on pupil behaviors. Anderson's work indicated that the teacher is the most influential agent in the classroom for determining the climate of the classroom. Based on this concept, the Withall system contains only teacher categories which are polarized along a teacher-centered, pupil-centered dimension.

The system is primarily affective; however, it does contain categories which separate problem-structuring statements (or questions) from neutral statements.

This system preceded the Flanders' System of Interaction Analysis, and contributed to the development of the teacher categories of the Flanders' System. The system can be used for providing feedback to teachers and to supervisors about the social-emotional climate being induced by a teacher.

The coding unit is a word or words, sentence or sentences containing an idea or theme and a dominant intent either to support the teacher and his behaviors or the learner and his behaviors. Complex statements may comprise several units.

The author suggests a minimum of 50 consecutive teacher or leader statements, questions or comments, but states that 200 is more desirable and may be collected during more than one class meeting.

## OBSERVER RELIABILITY PROCEDURES

Separate observers categorize and work independently to place identical statements into the same categories. Range of reliability reported by the author is .64 to .75.

## SUPPLEMENTARY MATERIALS

Withall, John. "The Development of a Technique for the Measurement of Social-Emotional Climate in Classrooms," Journal of Experimental Education, March 1949, Vol. XVII, pp. 347-361.
Withall, John. "Impact on Learners of Climate Created by the Teacher" (film), Bureau of Audio-Visual Instruction, University of Wisconsin, Madison, Wisconsin, 1963.

CATEGORIES FOR

SOCIAL-EMOTIONAL CLIMATE INDEX

John Withall

Criteria of Teacher-Statement Categories

1.  LEARNER SUPPORTIVE statements or questions

These are teacher-statements or questions that express agreement with the ideas, actions or opinions of the learner, or that commend or reassure the learner. Agreement is frequently expressed by a monosyllabic response such as "Yes," "Right," "Uhuhuh," and the like. Commendation or reassurance may be stated in terms of:

a.  class-accepted criteria or goals
    or
b.  the private goals and subjective criteria of the teacher.

The dominant intent of these statements or questions is to praise, encourage or bolster the learner.

2.  ACCEPTANT or CLARIFYING statements or questions

These are teacher-statements or questions which either:

a.  accept, that is, evidence considerable understanding by the teacher of,
    or
b.  clarify, that is, restate clearly and succinctly in the teacher's words

the ideational or the feeling content of the learner's statement. The dominant intent of these teacher-responses is to help the learner to gain insight into his problem, that is, define his "real" problem and its solution in more operational terms.

3.  PROBLEM-STRUCTURING statements or questions

Problem-structuring responses by the teacher offer facts or ideas or opinions to the learner about

                        a.   phenomena

                        b.   procedures

in a non-threatening and objective manner. These responses contain NO element of advising or recommending the adoption of certain ideas or procedures. Problem-structuring responses are frequently posed as questions which seek further information from the learner about the problem confronting him; or they may be statements which offer information to the learner about his problem. The learner is free to accept or to reject in part or in entirety the facts or opinions that are presented to him. Problem-structuring responses may be questions which the teacher asks (1) to further increase her own understanding of what the learner has said, or (2) to increase the precision of the learner's statement of the problem. Problem-structuring responses are problem-centered rather than either teacher or learner-centered; nevertheless, they do tend to sustain the learner by facilitating his problem-solving activities.

4. NEUTRAL statements evidencing no supportive intent

These statements are neither teacher-sustaining, nor learner-sustaining nor problem-centered. They constitute a small percentage of the total teacher-responses. These responses include statements in which the teacher: (1) questions herself aloud; (2) repeats verbatim a statement that the learner just made; (3) uses a polite formality, et cetera. Statements having to do with administrative procedure--the room in which the class will meet, the hour at which a conference will occur--(especially after consensus has been achieved), fall into this category.

5. DIRECTIVE statements or questions

These are teacher-statements or questions which advise the learner regarding a course of action or his future behavior and which narrowly limit his choice or offer to choice. These statements recommend to the learner the facts or procedures that the teacher proffers him. These statements or questions convey the impression to the learner that the teacher expects and hopes that he will follow her prompting and that she will approve if he does. The intent of these responses is to have the learner take up the teacher's point of view and pursue a course of action that she advocates.

6. REPROVING, DISAPPROVING or DISPARAGING statements or questions

By means of these statements a teacher may express complete or partial disapproval of the ideas, behavior, and, to her, personality weaknesses of the learner. The teacher's internalized societal values largely enter into these responses. By means of these statements some teachers believe they are fulfilling their responsibility of inculcating in young people society's standards of acceptable and desirable behavior and achievement. The intent of these statements is:

a. to represent to the learner societal values as the teacher sees them;

b. to admonish the learner for unacceptable behavior and to deter him from repeating it in the future;

c. to impress on the learner the fact that he has not met the criteria for successful achievement which the teacher accepts.

7. TEACHER-SUPPORTIVE statements or questions

These are statements or questions in which the teacher refers to herself and expresses a defensive attitude, or refers to her present or past interests, activities or possessions with the purpose of reassuring herself and of confirming her position or her ideas in the eyes of those around her. The dominant intent of these teacher-responses is to assert, to defend or to justify the teacher. Statements in which the teacher perseverates on an idea, a belief or a suggestion would fall in this category. By "perseveration" is meant a persisting in, a reiteration of, and a rigid advocacy of an idea or opinion by the teacher despite additional data being presented to her which calls for a re-examination of the original idea or opinion.

# A FRAME OF REFERENCE AND
## PROCEDURE TO FACILITATE CATEGORIZATION
## OF TEACHER-STATEMENTS

Each teacher-statement contains one of two dominant kinds of intent.  These are:

either a)  intent to sustain the teacher and his behavior
(teacher-centered statements)

or b)  intent to sustain the learner and his behavior
(learner-centered statements and issue-centered
statements are included under this intent).

By analysis of both the CONTEXT and the CONTENT of a teacher statement it may be possible to determine whether the dominant intent of a statement is to sustain the teacher or the learner.

Once the dominant intent of a teacher-statement has been ascertained, one can proceed to determine the technique by which the support is conveyed.

1.  If the statement is intended primarily to sustain the teacher,
one or possibly a combination of the two following techniques
may be used:

a)  reproof of the learner (category 6)

b)  directing or advising the learner (category 5).

Frequently the intent of the statement is to sustain the teacher yet neither of the above techniques is used.  In that event the statement is simply a self-supportive remark which defends the teacher or evidences perseveration in support of the teacher's position or ideas. (category 7)

2.  If the intent of a statement is to sustain the learner then one or possibly a combination of the two following techniques may be used:

a)  clarification and acceptance of the learner's feelings or ideas
(category 2),

b)  problem-structuring statements (category 3).

Frequently the intent of a statement is to sustain the learner yet neither of the above techniques is used.  In that event the statement is simply one that reassures, commends, agrees with or otherwise sustains the learner (category 1).

Infrequently a teacher-statement may have no dominant intent to sustain either the teacher or the learner.  If the statement represents neither of the techniques in the two intent areas nor gives evidence of being one of the more general kinds of supporting statements, then the statement can be considered to have no intent to support and should be placed in category 4.

Recourse to the learner-statement or behavior before and after a teacher response, particularly when one encounters a statement in which the intent is difficult to ascertain, is sometimes helpful in categorizing the teacher's statements.

Abstracted from

# TEACHER-PUPIL INTERACTION IN THE
# MATHEMATICS CLASSROOM*

A Sub-project Report of the Secondary
Mathematics Evaluation Project

E. Muriel J. Wright

**25**

*From Technical Report No. 67-5, Minnesota National Laboratory, Minnesota State Department of Education, May, 1967.

# WRIGHT SYSTEM SUMMARY

|  |  | SYSTEM DIMENSION |
|---|---|---|
| * | ** |  |
| X | 19 | Affective |
| X | 16 | Cognitive |
|  | 6 | Work process (control) |
|  | 4 | Behavior |

## TYPE OF COMMUNICATION RECORDED

| X | 25 | Verbal |
|---|---|---|
|  | 7 | Nonverbal |

## SUBJECT OF OBSERVATION

|  | 5 | Teacher only |
|---|---|---|
|  | 2 | Student only |
| X | 19 | Teacher and student |

## DATA COLLECTION METHODS REPORTED

| X | 18 | Live |
|---|---|---|
| X | 13 | Tape recording without tapescript |
|  | 9 | Tape recording and tapescript |
| X | 13 | Video tape |
|  | 1 | Handwritten notes |

## AUDIO OR VIDEO TAPE REQUIRED

|  | 9 | Yes |
|---|---|---|
| X | 17 | No |

## PERSONNEL NEEDED FOR OBSERVATION OR RECORDING SESSION

| X | 17 | 1 coder |
|---|---|---|
|  | 1 | Team of 2 |
|  | 1 | 2 teams of 2 |
|  | 9 | Tape operator |

## NUMBER OF CODERS NEEDED DURING CODING SESSION

| X | 17 | No coder other than observer(s) |
|---|---|---|
|  | 3 | 1 coder |
|  | 2 | 2 coders |
|  | 4 | 2 teams of 2 coders |

## CODING UNITS

| X | 18 | Category change |
|---|---|---|
|  | 9 | Category + time unit |
|  | 6 | Content area change |
|  | 3 | Speaker change |
|  | 3 | Time sample |

## USES REPORTED BY AUTHOR

| X | 26 | Research |
|---|---|---|
|  | 12 | Teacher training |
|  | 9 | Supervision |

* Summary of information for this system

** Summary of information for 26 systems

# THE MINNESOTA LABORATORY FIVE STATE SYSTEM

This system is an outgrowth of the Wright-Proctor system, and both systems are designed for use in mathematics classrooms.

An unusual aspect of this system is that it has an affective dimension which focuses on pupil involvement, by measuring how the teacher makes contact with the student. For instance, does he make contact only by checking with him in ways that invite limited participation, does he confront him in ways that invite extensive participation or does he make challenging or jolting statements in order to bring him in? Student categories include: responds passively or independently, moves to more steps than were raised by the teacher, brings in related topics to mathematics with a fresh approach.

The cognitive dimensions of the Wright instrument focus on both teacher and pupil behaviors in 3 areas: fundamentals, relationship and applications. This is a simplified version of the original Wright-Proctor instrument, which should make the system more easily usable by observers not trained in mathematics.

The affective dimension of the Wright instrument is applicable for assessing pupil involvement in classrooms studying any subject matter.

## OBSERVER RELIABILITY PROCEDURES

Inter-observer agreement is determined by use of the Scott coefficient. Kinescopes were classified by all observers and comparison of individual and mean scores were made. The author reports a range of reliability scores for involvement of .49 to .90 and for content of .40 to .85.

## SUPPLEMENTARY MATERIALS

Wright, Muriel J. "Teacher Pupil Interaction in the Mathematics Classroom." Observer's Manual, Appendix No. 1, Technical Report No. 67-5, Minnesota National Laboratory, Minnesota State Department of Education, May, 1967.

CATEGORIES FOR
MINNESOTA NATIONAL LABORATORY FIVE STATE SYSTEM

E. Muriel J. Wright

CONTENT CATEGORIES
(both teacher and pupils behaviors)
(viewed in terms of all categories)


## FUNDAMENTALS

1. <u>Structure:</u>
examination of "old" knowledge as an end in itself, as in a review; or a clearcut break during development of a new relation or during application of new or old concepts.

2. <u>Techniques:</u>
while techniques already mastered are in constant use, this category is only to be used when the effect of the behavior is the use or the "how" of old knowledge as an end in itself, such as in a drill or review, or as a clearcut break during development of a new relation or during application of new or old concepts, i.e. a shift in the concern from the new relation or from the particular concepts being applied to preoccupation with the procedures involved.


## RELATIONS

3. <u>Deductive:</u>
the formal proof of a new concept

4. <u>Inductive:</u>
the informal examination or discovery of a new concept

5. <u>Statement:</u>
the statement of a new concept


## APPLICATIONS

6. <u>Mathematical:</u>
the use of, or practice with, new or old concepts in problems of purely mathematical nature

7. <u>Other:</u>
the use or place of new or old concepts of mathematics in other subjects or in discussion of the development of mathematics historically

FUNDAMENTALS: The body of mathematical knowledge at the command of the pupils: 'old' knowledge up to an arbitrary cut off point which changes regularly and must be clearly defined in each study. In the Five State Project where observation can rarely occur on consecutive days, "work covered before today" may be the most practical cut off. In practice the observer will modify this where previous work has obviously not been mastered by most of the class.

FUNDAMENTALS - Structure: The examination or the why of 'old' knowledge as an end in itself, as in a review; or as a clearcut break during development of a new relation or during application of new or old concepts.

- Fundamental elements, operations, postulates.
- Well established theory when understanding is apparent--to include definitions, notation, theorems.
- Logical principles--to include consistency, equivalence, proof.
- Strategies of problem solving, e. g. verification of facts, varying of conditions, testing hypotheses, inventing analogous problems, estimation of plausible answers, analysis of a method of problem solving.

FUNDAMENTALS - Techniques: While techniques already mastered are in constant use, this category is only to be used when the effect of the behavior is the use or the 'how' of old knowledge as an end in itself, such as in a drill or review, or as a clearcut break during development of a new relation or during application of new or old concepts, i. e. a shift in the concern from the new relation or from the particular concepts being applied to preoccupation with the procedures involved.

- Extensive use of well mastered processes, which will certainly vary from grade to grade, e. g. multiplication in grade 8; use of quadratic formula in a senior algebra class to determine roots; use of square root tables in a probability class.
- Reading of mathematical materials, e. g. answers or even solutions to homework problems where no evidence of immediate development of the solution, assignment of homework, reading, from text, first reading of a problem when no emphasis is made of specific conditions.
- In contrast to FUNDAMENTALS - Structure which probes or examines mastered knowledge, and to the categories of RELATIONS which describe activity in building new concepts, and to the categories of APPLICATION which applies concepts to particular problems, the category of FUNDAMENTALS - Techniques might be viewed as somewhat weak, or static, or routine <u>albeit essential</u> for the progress of the lesson.

RELATIONS:   The development, formal or informal,
and the statement of new knowledge.


RELATIONS - Deductive:   The formal proof of a new concept.

- The complete formal proof or any parts of such a proof.
- Logical discussion in search of a formal proof as might occur in analysis of the
  newly stated concept or consideration of available knowledge that might be adapted to the solution of this general problem.


RELATIONS - Inductive:   The informal examination or discovery of a new concept.

- By use of a variety of specific examples selected to elicit new generalization or
  juxtaposition, e. g. problems used for this purpose may begin quite simply and
  rapidly increase in technical complexity until the pupils begin to look beyond the
  old methods for a more powerful  new method or note a common characteristic
  that may summarize the complete family of problems presented to them.
- Use of an example to make a formally stated relation clear.


RELATIONS - Statement:   The statement of a new concept.

- May occur before, after or during either formal or informal examination
  of a new concept.
- May be used to classify a teacher's encouragement of statement of a concept as
  well as either teacher or pupils' actual statement.
- May be right or wrong - can be subsequently accepted or rejected.
- Definitions, notations, terminology, mathematical conventions when dealing
  with new material.
- Should be reserved for clearcut statement (or encouragement of this by teacher)
  of the generalized concept.

APPLICATIONS: The use or place of the mathematical system in specific problems and in other fields and in historical context.

APPLICATIONS - Mathematical: The use of, or practice with, new or old concepts in problems of purely mathematical nature.

- May occur in "drill" type exercises.
- May occur in the "word" problems.
- May occur during the solution of the mathematical part of problems drawn from some other area, e. g. physics, economics, biology...

APPLICATIONS - Other: The use or place of new or old concepts of mathematics in other subjects or in discussion of the development of the mathematics historically.

- Examination of the 1-1 correspondence between a specific physical situation and a mathematical system.
- Brief statement of a problem in another field before beginning selection of aspects for mathematical solution and final statement of solution as it applies to the other field.
- Examination of a problem in terms of the concepts of the other field, e. g. two solutions to mathematical aspects of the problem, one positive one negative might be reduced to one realistic solution in the physical situation.
- Mention of mathematicians contributing to development of specific concepts.
- Consideration of modification of concept, e. g. idea of 'limit' from Archimedes to modern times.

## PUPIL INVOLVEMENT CATEGORIES

**T E A C H E R**

1. Clarifying, encouraging, summarizing:
   remarks which recognize student, his participation and ideas by incorporating them into classroom interaction.

2. Contacting, checking:
   remarks, usually questions, which invite limited participation: asking for information, simple next steps or checking student understanding.

3. Confronting, seeking:
   remarks, usually questions, which invite extensive participation: classifying information, a series of steps, a single step requiring selection and organization of material.

4. Soft or hard challenging, jolting:
   remarks absurd, controversial or questions of comprehensive nature or completely undirected to invite significant participation:
   in noting relationships, application, in making grand leaps in system development.

5. Informing, lecturing:
   remarks, expository, to provide information or solve problems;
   also rhetorical questions. These may be continued into a "lecture" period or be met in rapid discussion. Reading answers.

6. Directing:
   remarks assigning particular tasks related to the lesson:
   homework assignment, a method of recording data, a type of material to use.

**P U P I L**

7. Receptive, passive:
   remarks by student under direction limited to one-step answers, or trivial agreement or question initiated without readiness to treat it himself. Reading book or answers.

8. Independent, active:
   remarks by student either as invited and moving more than one step ahead, or a single powerful step, or without invitation to raise a question and being willing to treat it himself.

9. Curious, creative:
   remarks by student in which present topic related to other areas of mathematics or to applied fields, to more fundamental concepts, or to a wider family of topics. A fresh topic related to present topic.

**G E N E R A L**

O. Silence, confusion, organization:
   behaviors concerned with lesson which cannot be classified 1-9

8 - Wright

# EXAMPLES OF CLASSIFICATION OF VERBAL BEHAVIOR IN CATEGORIES FOR PUPIL INVOLVEMENT

1. Clarifying, Encouraging, Summarizing
    1.1  Statements in recognition of pupil's comment.
    1.2  Answers to pupil's question.
    1.3  Explaining and amplifying a pupil's answer.
    1.4  Encouragement of pupil in developing his own idea.
    1.5  Restatement of pupil's answer.
    1.6  Praise or comment in response to a pupil's statement, answer or question.

2. Contacting, Checking
    2.1  Simple passive question requiring a simple passive response.
    2.2  Question anticipating simple one-step or trivial answers.
    2.3  Question where range of possible answers is narrow.
    2.4  Drill.
    2.5  Request for information requiring simple recall or request for mere reading from text or notes.
    2.6  Checking pupil's understanding, e.g., "Any questions," "Difficulty anyone."

3. Confronting, Seeking
    3.1  Statements requiring extensive participation.
    3.2  Questions requiring independent thought.
    3.3  A one-step answer but requiring selection and organization of material.
    3.4  Statement eliciting pupil criticism of own work.
    3.5  Broad questions demanding responses similar to 3.1 and 3.2 but where direction less clearly specified.

4. Soft or hard Challenging, Jolting
    4.1  Questions requiring very deep understanding.
    4.2  Controversial questions of comprehensive nature.
    4.3  Questions requiring understanding leading to relationships, applications, or grand leaps in system development.
    4.4  Absurd statements requiring deep understanding by pupils.
    4.5  Undirected questions inviting significant participation at a high level of understanding.
    4.6  Statements requiring elaboration on difficult homework.

5. Informing, Lecturing
    5.1  Expression of opinions or facts relating to mathematics.
    5.2  Teacher talk, but not inviting participation.
    5.3  Rhetorical questions and answers.
    5.4  Reading answers to problems (place B with it).
    5.5. Reading problems or information from book (place B with it).

6. Directing
    6.1  Express statements or questions requiring delayed pupil response.
    6.2  Entire direction and explanations of assignment.
    6.3  Instructions on use of materials.

7. Receptive, Passive
    7.1   Pupil response to simple questions.
    7.2   Trivial statements, comments, responses.
    7.3   Simple question without being able to treat it himself.
    7.4   Drill.
    7.5   Reading a problem from book (place B beside it).
    7.6   Reading answers to problems (place B beside it).
    7.7   Information of simple recall nature including answers to homework assignment.

8. Independent, Active
    8.1   Answers to difficult questions requiring multiple-step solutions.
    8.2   Statements made by pupil indicating powerful step or deep understanding.
    8.3   Responses demonstrating selection or organization of material.
    8.4   Suggestions of independent nature given without specific request to explain difficult points.

9. Curious, Creative
    9.1   High-level comments showing definite insight.
    9.2   Pupil voluntarily relates the material to other areas of mathematics or to applied fields.
    9.3   Pupil presents a fresh topic related to the topic under discussion.
    9.4   An elegant solution suggested through pupil understanding (not from books).
    9.5   Unusual application of topic.
    9.6   Unusual generalizations.
    9.7   Originality.
    9.8   Humor related to subject matter.

O. Silence, Confusion, Organization
    0.1   The first and last entry in each daily classification to ensure totals in matrix are balanced.
    0.2   Writing on board or writing at seats during main lesson unaccompanied by explanatory comment (place B beside it).
    0.3   Recording of data, homework, grades, etc.

Abstracted from

# SYSTEMATIC OBSERVATION OF VERBAL INTERACTION AS A METHOD OF COMPARING MATHEMATICS LESSONS*

## Appendix B: A Self Training Manual

E. Muriel J. Wright
Virginia Proctor

*Published by Washington University, St. Louis, June, 1961.
The research was performed pursuant to a contract with the United States Office of Health, Education and Welfare, under the provisions of the Cooperative Research Program, Project #816.

# WRIGHT-PROCTOR SYSTEM SUMMARY

### SYSTEM DIMENSION

| * | ** | |
|---|----|--|
| X | 19 | Affective |
| X | 16 | Cognitive |
|   | 6  | Work process (control) |
|   | 4  | Behavior |

### TYPE OF COMMUNICATION RECORDED

| | | |
|---|----|--|
| X | 25 | Verbal |
|   | 7  | Nonverbal |

### SUBJECT OF OBSERVATION

| | | |
|---|----|--|
|   | 5  | Teacher only |
|   | 2  | Student only |
| X | 19 | Teacher and student |

### DATA COLLECTION METHODS REPORTED

| | | |
|---|----|--|
| X | 18 | Live |
| X | 13 | Tape recording without tapescript |
|   | 9  | Tape recording and tapescript |
| X | 13 | Video tape |
|   | 1  | Handwritten notes |

### AUDIO OR VIDEO TAPE REQUIRED

| | | |
|---|----|--|
|   | 9  | Yes |
| X | 17 | No |

### PERSONNEL NEEDED FOR OBSERVATION OR RECORDING SESSION

| | | |
|---|----|--|
| X | 17 | 1 coder |
|   | 1  | Team of 2 |
|   | 1  | 2 teams of 2 |
|   | 9  | Tape operator |

### NUMBER OF CODERS NEEDED DURING CODING SESSION

| | | |
|---|----|--|
| X | 17 | No coder other than observer(s) |
|   | 3  | 1 coder |
|   | 2  | 2 coders |
|   | 4  | 2 teams of 2 coders |

### CODING UNITS

| | | |
|---|----|--|
| X | 18 | Category change |
|   | 9  | Category + time unit |
|   | 6  | Content area change |
|   | 3  | Speaker change |
|   | 3  | Time sample |

### USES REPORTED BY AUTHOR

| | | |
|---|----|--|
| X | 26 | Research |
|   | 12 | Teacher training |
|   | 9  | Supervision |

* Summary of information for this system

** Summary of information for 26 systems

# THE WRIGHT-PROCTOR SYSTEM

This category system was designed for use in the mathematics classroom only. It was developed in order to determine whether teachers were teaching new math curriculum in ways that were essentially different from the ways that they taught the old math curriculum. Although it seems reasonable that basic revisions in curriculum would produce changes in the way the teachers interact with the students, to date, this has not proved to be true in the affective domain. Work with the Wright-Proctor system indicates that this may be the case with respect to certain cognitive dimensions that teachers work with. This classification system requires an observer who is trained both in this system and who is familiar with the content of mathematics, thus making it a difficult system to learn to use.

## OBSERVER RELIABILITY PROCEDURES

Rough check by graphing on binomial probability paper. Use of chi-squared comparisons of proportions at $P = .05$. Rank order comparisons of triple classifications. The author reports the range of reliability scores at $P = .05$ or smaller.

## SUPPLEMENTARY MATERIALS

Wright, E. M. and Proctor, V. H. Systematic Observation of Verbal Interaction as a Method of Comparing Mathematics Lessons. Under cooperative Research Project No. 816, U.S. Office of Education, Dept. of Health, Education, and Welfare. St. Louis: Washington University, June, 1961.

E. M. Wright and V. Proctor

## CLASSIFICATION OF VERBAL BEHAVIORS:  IN THE FRAME CONTENT

<u>Fundamentals</u>    The body of mathematical knowledge at the command of the pupils;  'old' knowledge up to arbitrary cut off point such as last chapter or topic.

1. Structure
   1.1  Fundamental elements, operations, postulates
   1.2  Well established theory when understanding is apparent, e. g. definitions, suitable notation, theorems
   1.3  Logical principles, e. g. consistency, inference, equivalence, proof
   1.4  Strategies of problem solving, e. g. verification of facts, varying of conditions, testing hypotheses, inventing analogous problems, estimation of plausible answers, analysis of a method of problem solving

2. Techniques
   2.1  Description and use of mechanical processes or rules where basic mathematical relation is not made apparent, e. g. mechanical use of tables
   2.2  Reading of mathematical materials already developed, e. g. answers to home-work problems, assignment of homework, first reading of a problem with no emphasis of specific conditions

<u>Relations</u>    The development and statement of 'new' relations

3. Deductive
   3.1  Logical proof of new theory

4. Inductive
   4.1  Use of specific examples selected to elicit new generalization or relation, e. g. problems used for this purpose usually begin quite simply and increase in technical complexity until pupils begin to look beyond the old method or for a new solution or for a general relationship
   4.2  Use of graphs, diagrams to make a relation clear
   4.3  Intuitive approach to a relation, e. g. "What seems to be true?"

5. Statement
   5.1  Statements of new relations; may or may not be developed deductively or in-ductively; may be used in seeking method of problem solution in recent application, e. g. the statement may be right or wrong, may be pulled out for examination, and subsequently proved or disproved
   5.2  Definitions, notation, terminology; mathematical conventions e. g. selection of means of describing empirical data such as means, mode, median, measures of dispersion, type of graphs in statistics

<u>Applications</u>    The use, place of the mathematical system in specific problems and in historical context

6. Mathematical

7.  Other
    7.1 Brief statement of problem in other field before abstraction essentials
    7.2 Examination of problems in terms of the concepts of the other field
    7.3 References from mathematical history
    7.4 Reference to new topics or different treatment to be met in later courses
    7.5 Humor--when pertinent to mathematical activities

NEGATIVE behaviors are recorded when clearly false statement of mathematical content is made.  If the observer is in doubt in the context, behavior is classed positive.

# CLASSIFICATION OF VERBAL BEHAVIORS:  IN THE FRAME PROCESS

Syllogistic          The syllogistic categories of analyzing and synthesizing require the logical operation of inference.  Although synthesizing is often mechanical it may also be the method of highly creative divergent thinking.

1.  Analyzing -- from assumption of desired conclusion toward accepted principles
    1.1  Chain of backward implication -- "is implied by"
    1.2  Less systematic moving backward from goal seeking connection with known premises to establish approach to proof
    1.3  Justification of a statement, e. g.  Why? Because...;  plausibility
    1.4  Moving backward over an argument to discover mistake or clarify meaning

2.  Synthesizing -- from accepted principles toward desired conclusion
    2.1  Chain of forward implication -- "implies," e.g., when moving forward from known premises to goal, synthesizing may be mechanical when method is a familiar one;  formal development or proof of theory or specific problem; reading entire proof already developed carefully step by step
    2.2  Consolidation of parts into a complete solution

Classificatory   The classificatory categories of generalizing and specializing include the formulation of generalizations, their applications, and the less formal but very necessary heuristic process of problem dissection and focusing on goal.

3.  Specializing -- the use of significant attributes of a given set in an analogous set, or the application of a given set in a smaller included set
    3.1  Selection of significant parts of a problem -- dissection, abstraction, e. g. verification of facts of problem;  identification of necessary and sufficient conditions;  identification of true and false statements
    3.2  Application of a generalization, e. g. substitution in a formula, use of theorem, definition
    3.3  Recognition of relation of corresponding sets, e. g. analogous problems
    3.4  Focusing on goal, e. g., recentering on goal at successive phases of solution

4.  Generalizing -- the recognition of significant attributes of a given set and the passing from the consideration of the given set to that of a larger inclusive set.
    4.1  Recognizing significant attributes and passing to a larger set, e. g. moving from particular examples to a common characteristic, a good guess, a hypothesis, the formulation of a problem, of a definition
    4.2  Statement of a formula, law, relation, definition to be proved or arising from development or to be examined for meaning

Relevant          A more static category, the statement of relevant information occurs when mathematical information is presented but belongs to no apparent logical sequence.

5.  Relevant
    5.1  Information about specific mathematics, e. g. problem read from book, reading of homework answers when no solution meaning given
    5.2  Information about more general aspects of mathematics, e. g. historical, biographical without logical analysis of the mathematical ideas that may thus be referred to

NEGATIVE behaviors are recorded when reasoning is invalid.

# CLASSIFICATION OF VERBAL BEHAVIORS:  IN THE FRAME ATTITUDE

<u>Teacher or Pupil</u>   The teacher demonstrates or encourages pupils behaviors in each category;  the pupils demonstrate the behaviors in each category.

1. Curiosity -- fresh unusual material;  a new direction
   1.1 Teacher statements relating present topic to other areas of mathematics or to other fields, or to more fundamental mathematical concepts or to historical context
   1.2 Teacher encouragement of unusual problem or new direction including positive support of pupil expression of unusual interest
   1.3 Pupils make statements as in 1.1
   1.4 Pupils ask questions about 1.1

2. Independence
   2.1 Teacher open questions or suggestions demanding pupil thinking beyond one carefully structured step, e.g. asking pupils to solve problems, asking pupils to discuss homework answers, asking pupil suggestion for relation apparent in a series of specific examples, requiring pupil development of proof of a relation, eliciting pupil criticism of his own work
   2.2 Turning of pupil-raised question back to same pupil or to the class
   2.3 Assignment of pupil topics for class demonstration including regular homework questions developed on blackboard by pupil
   2.4 Pupil statements moving problem solution forward more than one step during the interval
   2.5 Responsibility for development taken by pupil sometimes indicated by several steps forward or merely by one powerful step forward in a single interval
   2.6 Pupil initiates discussion by asking a question and noting specific aspects he has considered

3. Receptivity

   3.1 Teacher tells, states, solves problems
   3.2 Teacher asks rhetorical questions or questions limited to one-step often trivial or merely yes-no answers
   3.3 Teacher is responsive to signals that pupils understand, follow the discussion, are interested in the presentation
   3.4 Pupils respond appropriately when called on, but answer is limited to one relatively small step, e.g., "I don't know." "The square of 7 is 49." "Yes." "The answer to that homework question was x plus 2."
   3.5 Pupils ask questions without indicating readiness to treat it themselves with teacher's assistance, e.g., "How do you do this problem?" "I couldn't solve number 37."

NEGATIVE behaviors are recorded when discouragement is apparent either in teacher or pupils.

INDEX OF INITIATIVE:  Although each behavior can be classed in only one of the categories of Attitude, unlike the other two frames, the categories are related serially: Curiosity presupposes Independence and Independence presupposes Receptivity.  This relationship of categories makes reasonable an Index of Initiative by a simple weighting of the positive behaviors in each category.  This is discussed in Project 816 and in this Manual under Treatment of data-comparison.

# CLASSIFICATION OF OTHER BEHAVIORS: NEUTRAL AND NON-VERBAL

## Neutral

Verbal behaviors which concern non-mathematical matters are classified as Neutral. Examples of these are classroom organization behaviors, disciplinary comments, interruptions by school administration such as announcements over the public address system, inactivity or the occasional group bedlam.

## Silent study

Mathematical study occurs in the classroom silently in several ways.
1. Short periods of silence may comprise a complete interval set aside for classification of class interaction. 2. Within the general discussion period, the teacher may direct that all the pupils individually, at their seats or with some at the blackboard, should develop a point for immediate use in class discussion. 3. Preceding or following the general class discussion the pupils may have a work period in which they may be doing assignments with individual pupils conferring with the teacher. 4. Tests of short duration-- over the course, say, of ten minutes-- may occur. Where tests require the entire class period no observation would be made.

These several types of silent study may be classified as S 1, 2, 3, 4 if it is found useful to differentiate them. Indeed in the cases of S 1 and S 2, the observer may be able to infer as well as in verbal discussion the behaviors being demonstrated by the pupils. If it is important in a given study, these two types, may in addition to the S classification, be noted in terms of the appropriate categories of content, process and attitude as if the behavior had been overt. e. g. S 1 (P 622)

# TRIPLE VIEWPOINT OF THE WRIGHT-PROCTOR INSTRUMENT

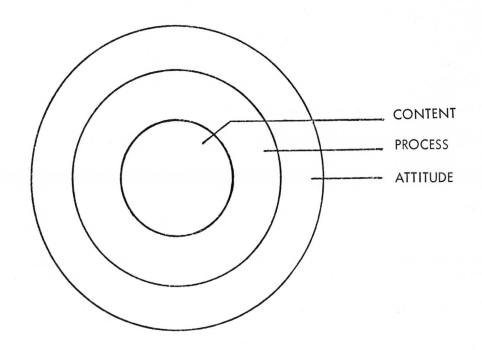

CONTENT

PROCESS

ATTITUDE

| MATHEMATICAL CONTENT | PSYCHOLOGICAL PROCESS | SOCIOLOGICAL ATTITUDE |
|---|---|---|
| Structure ⎤<br>Techniques ⎦ Fundamentals<br><br>Deductive ⎤<br>Inductive ⎥ Relations<br>Statements ⎦<br><br>Mathematical ⎤<br>Other ⎦ Applications | Analyzing ⎤<br>Synthesizing ⎦ Syllogistic<br><br>Specializing ⎤<br>Generalizing ⎦ Classificatory<br>Relevant | Curiosity<br>Independence<br>Receptivity |

# SECTION THREE

## BIBLIOGRAPHY
## AND
## INDEX

# BIBLIOGRAPHY

Agazarian, Yvonne, and Simon, Anita. "Sequential Analysis of Verbal Interaction, Concepts I." Part I of a series of three papers presented at the Annual Convention of the American Association of Humanistic Psychology, New York, September, 1966.

——. "Sequential Analysis of Verbal Interaction, Mechanics I." Part II, ibid.

Amidon, Edmund. "Interaction Analysis: Recent Developments." Paper presented at the American Educational Research Association convention, Chicago, February, 1966.

——. "Using Interaction Analysis at Temple University." Paper read at the Conference on the Implications of Recent Research on Teaching for Teacher Education, sponsored by the National Association for Student Teaching and the University of Rochester, Rochester, New York, January, 1966.

——. "A Technique for Analyzing Counselor — Counselee Interaction." In James Adams (Ed.), Counseling and Guidance: A Summary View. New York: Macmillan Company, 1965, 50-56.

Amidon, Edmund J., and Flanders, Ned A. The Role of the Teacher in the Classroom. Minneapolis, Minnesota: Association for Productive Teaching, Inc., 1967. (Revised Edition).

——. "The Effects of Direct and Indirect Teacher Influence on Dependent-Prone Students Learning Geometry." J. Ed. Psychol., 1961, 52:286-91.

Amidon, Edmund, Furst, Norma, and Mickelson, J. "The Effects of Teaching Interaction Analysis to Student Teachers." Paper presented at the American Educational Research Association convention, New York, February, 1967.

Amidon, Edmund, Furst, Norma, Moskowitz, Gertrude, and Simon, Anita. "An Experimental Course in Pre-Service Education." In Anita Simon (Ed.) Classroom Interaction Newsletter, Vol. I, No. 2, Philadelphia, May, 1966.

Amidon, Edmund, and Giammatteo, Michael. "The Verbal Behavior of Superior Teachers." The Elem. Sch. J., February, 1965, 65:283-85.

Amidon, Edmund J., and Hunter, Elizabeth. Improving Teaching: Analyzing Verbal Interaction in the Classroom. New York: Holt, Rinehart, and Winston, 1966.

Amidon, Edmund, Kies, Kathleen, and Palisi, Anthony. "Group Supervision." Nat'l. Elem. Prin., April, 1966, 45:54-58.

Amidon, Edmund, and Simon, Anita. "Implications for Teacher Education of Interaction Analysis Research in Student Teaching." Paper presented at the annual convention of the American Educational Research Association, Chicago, February, 1965.

——. "Teacher-Pupil Interaction." Rev. Ed. Res. 1965, 35:130-39.

Anderson, C. C., and Hunka, S. M. "Teacher Evaluation: Some Problems and a Proposal." Harvard Ed. Rev., 1963, 33:74-95.

Anderson, Harold H. "A Study of Certain Criteria of Teaching Effectiveness." J. of Exp. Ed., September, 1964; 23:41-71.

——. "Domination and Socially Integrative Behavior." In R. G. Barker, J. S. Kounin, and H. F. Wright (Eds.) Child Behavior and Development. New York: McGraw-Hill, 1943.

——. "The Measurement of Domination and of Socially Integrative Behavior in Teachers' Contacts with Children." Chld. Devlpm., 1939; 10:73-89.

——. "An Experimental Study of Dominative and Integrative Behavior in Children of Pre-School Age." J. Soc. Psychol., 1937; 8:335-345.

——. "Domination and Integration in the Social Behavior of Young Children in an Experimental Play Situation." Genet. Psychol. Monogr., 1937; 19:341-408.

Anderson, Harold, and Brewer, Helen. "Studies of Teachers' Classroom Personalities, I: Dominative and Socially Integrative Behavior of Kindergarten Teachers." Psychol. Monogr. No. 6, 1945.

Anderson, Harold, and Brewer, J. E. "Studies of Teachers' Classroom Personalities, II: Effects of Teachers' Dominative and Integrative Contacts on Children's Classroom Behavior." Psychol. Monogr., No. 8, 1946.

Anderson, Harold, Brewer, J. E., and Reed, Mary F. "Studies of Teachers' Classroom Personalities, III: Follow-up Studies of the Effects of Dominative and Integrative Contacts on Children's Behavior." Psychol. Monogr., No. 11, 1946.

Anderson, J. P. "Student Perception of Teacher Influence." Unpublished doctoral dissertation, University of Minnesota, Minneapolis, 1960.

Anderson, John. "Conclusions Concerning Teaching Influence, Pupil Attitudes and Achievement." Paper presented at the American Educational Research Association annual convention, Chicago, February, 1963.

Armstrong, Jenny R. "A Theoretical Model for Research in Education." Paper presented at the annual meeting of the American Educational Research Association, New York, February, 1967.

Aschner, Mary Jane. "The Analysis of Classroom Discourse: A Method and Its Uses." Unpublished doctoral dissertation, University of Illinois, Urbana, 1959.

——. "The Analysis of Verbal Interaction in the Classroom." In Arno Bellack (Ed.) Theory and Research in Teaching. New York: Bureau of Publications, Teachers College, Columbia University, 1961. pp. 53-78.

——. "The Productive Thinking of the Gifted Children in the Classroom." Paper presented at the American Educational Research Association annual convention, Chicago, February, 1961.

Aschner, Mary Jane, Gallagher, James, et al. "A System for Classifying Thought Processes in the Context of Classroom Verbal Interaction." Institute for Research on Exceptional Children, University of Illinois, 1965.

Baker, Robert, and Wright, H. F. One Boy's Day. New York: Harper, 1951.

Bales, Robert F. "Conceptual Frameworks for Analysis of Social Interaction." J. Exp. Ed.,
June, 1962; 30 (No. 4), 323-24.

——. "Some Statistical Problems in Small Group Research." J. Amer. Statist. Assn., 1951;
46:311-22.

——. Interaction Process Analysis. Reading, Mass: Addison-Wesley, 1950.

——. "A Set of Categories for the Analysis of Small Group Interaction." Amer. Sociol. Rev.,
1950; 15:257-63.

Bales, R. F., and Gerbrands, H. "The Interaction Recorder; an Apparatus and Check List
for Sequential Content Analysis of Social Interaction." Hum. Rel., 1948; 1:456-63.

Bales, R. F., and Strodtbeck, F. L. "Phases in Group Problem Solving." J. Abnorm. Soc.
Psychol., 1951; 46:458-96.

Barr, A. S., et al. "Wisconsin Studies of the Measurement and Prediction of Teacher Effectiveness: A Summary of Investigations." Madison, Wisconsin: Denbar Publications.
1961.

Barr, Avril. Characteristic Differences in the Teaching Performance of Good and Poor
Teachers of Social Studies. Illinois: Public School Publishing Company, 1929.

Barr, Avril, Eustice, David, and Noe, Edward. "The Measurement and Prediction of
Teacher Efficiency." Rev. Ed. Res., June, 1955; 25:261-69.

Beiderman, David D. "Relationship Between Teaching Style and Pupil Behavior." Dissert.
Abstr., Dec. 1964; 25:3320.

Bellack, Arno A., et al. "The Language of the Classroom." USOE Cooperative Research
Project. Teachers College, Columbia University, New York, 1966.

Bellack, Arno. (Ed.) Theory and Research in Teaching. New York: Bureau of Publications,
Teachers College, Columbia University, 1963.

Bellack, A., and Huebner, D. "Teaching." Rev. Ed. Res., 1960; 30:246-57.

Bennett, Roger V. "Interrelationships Among Curricular, Social and Affective Dimensions
of the Teaching-Learning Act." Paper presented at the American Educational Research
Association convention, New York, February, 1967.

Berlin, J. I., and Wyckoff, B. "The Teaching of Improved Interpersonal Relations Through
Programmed Instruction for Two People Working Together." Paper presented at the
annual meeting of The American Psychological Association, Philadelphia, 1963.

Biddle, B. J., and Ellena, W. J. (Eds.) "Contemporary Research on Teacher Effectiveness."
New York: Holt, Rinehart, and Winston, 1964.

Bloom, Benjamin S., and Krathwohl, D. R. Taxonomy of Educational Objectives: Book I,
Cognitive Domain. New York: McKay, 1956.

Bowie, B. L., and Morgan, H. G. "Personal Values and Verbal Behavior of Teachers." J. Exp. Ed., 1962; 30:337-45.

Bowers, Norman D., and Soar, Robert S. "The Influence of Teacher Personality on Classroom Interaction." J. Exp. Ed., June, 1962; 30:309-11.

——. "Studies of Human Relations in the Teaching-Learning Process, V. Final Report." Evaluation of Laboratory Human Relations Training for Classroom Teachers. USOE Cooperative Research Project No. 469, 1961.

Boyd, R. D., and Devault, M. V. "The Observation and Recording of Behavior." Rev. Ed. Res., 1966; 36:529-551.

Boyer, E. Gil. Getting Research into Action. New York: Communication Materials Center, Inc., 1962.

Brode, E. Leland. "Imitation of Supervisors as a Factor in Teachers' Classroom Behavior." Paper presented at the American Educational Research Association convention, New York, February, 1967.

Browde, Joseph Arthur. "Patterns of Teacher Influence in Selected Church School Classrooms." In Anita Simon (Ed.) Classroom Interaction Newsletter, Vol. III, No. 1. Philadelphia, December, 1967.

Brookover, Wilbur B. "Person-Person Interaction Between Teachers and Pupils and Teaching Effectiveness." J. Ed. Res., December, 1940: 272-87.

Brown, George. "The Relationships Between Categories of Behavior of Third Grade Teachers." J. Ed. Res., May, 1961; 54:338-44.

Bush, R. N. The Teacher-Pupil Relationship. New York: Prentice-Hall. 1954.

Castetter, D. D., Standlee, L. S., and Fattu, N. A. "Teacher Effectiveness." Bulletin of the Inst. Ed. Res., 1 (No. 1), 1954.

Christensen, C. N. "Relationship Between Pupil Achievement, Pupil Affect-Need, Teacher Warmth, and Teacher Permissiveness." J. Ed. Psychol. 1960, 51:169-74.

Clements, Robert. "Art Teacher-Student Questioning and Dialogue in the Classroom." In Anita Simon (Ed.) Classroom Interaction Newsletter, Vol. II, No. 2, Philadelphia, May, 1967.

Coats, W. D. "Investigation and Simulation of the Relationships Among Selected Classroom Variables." USOE Cooperative Research Project No. 6-8330. Unpublished doctoral dissertation, University of Michigan, 1966.

Cogan, M. L. "Research on the Behavior of Teachers: A New Phase." Teach. Ed., 1963; 14:238-43.

——. "The Relation of the Behavior of Teachers to the Productive Behavior of Their Pupils." J. Exp. Ed., 1958; 27:89-124.

——. "Theory and Design of a Study of Teacher-Pupil Interaction." Harvard Ed. Rev., 1956; 26:315-342.

Collins, M. "Untrained and Trained Graduate Teachers: A Comparison of Their Experiences During the Probationary Year." Brit. J. Ed. Psychol., 1964; 34:75-84.

Cook, R. P., Reiter, S., and Cobabe, T. "Results of Classroom Observational Categories Within a Communication Model." (mimeograph), University of Wisconsin Research Project, Madison, Wisconsin.

Davidson, Roscoe L. "The Effects of An Interaction Analysis System on the Development of Critical Reading in Elementary School Children." Unpublished doctoral dissertation, University of Denver, 1967.

Davies, Lillian S. "Some Relationships Between Attitudes, Personality Characteristics, and Verbal Behavior of Selected Teachers." Unpublished doctoral dissertation, University of Minnesota, 1961.

Dawson, Richard William. Observer Reliability and the Classification of Classroom Communication. Minneapolis: University of Minnesota, 1962.

DeCharms, R., and Bridgement, W. J. "The Teaching-Learning Process Seen as a Problem in Interaction." Paper presented at American Educational Research Association meeting, Washington University, St. Louis, 1961.

Denny, David A. "A Preliminary Analysis of an Observation Schedule Designed to Identify the Teacher-Classroom Variables which Facilitate Pupil Creative Growth." Paper presented at the American Educational Research Association convention, New York, February, 1967.

Dixon, W. R. and Morse, W. C. "The Prediction of Teaching Performance; Empathic Potential." J. Teach. Ed., 1961; 12:322-9.

Dodl, Norman R. "Pupil Questioning Behavior in the Context of Classroom Interaction." Dissert. Abstr., May, 1966. 26:6441-42. (Revision of Flanders).

Dollins, Joseph C., et al. "With Words of Praise." El. Sch. J., 1960; 60:446-50.

Domas, S. J., and Tiedeman, D. V. "Teacher Competence: An Annotated Bibliography." J. Exp. Ed., 1950; 19:101-218.

Dyak, A. J. "Children's Social Interaction at School: A Comparison of Teachers and Classmates." In R. G. Barker (Ed.) The Stream of Behavior. New York: Appleton-Century Crofts. 1963.

Ellis, J. R. "Relationships Between Aspects of Preparation and Measures of Performance of Secondary Teachers of the Social Studies." J. Ed. Res., 1961; 55:24-8.

Enochs, Paul D. "An Experimental Study of a Method for Developing Creative Thinking in Fifth-Grade Children." Dissert. Abstr. February, 1965; 25:4538-39.

Evans, N. M. "Annotated Bibliography of British Research on Teaching and Teaching Ability." Ed. R's, Nov., 1961; 4:67-80.

Farrow, Ralph. "Changes in Student Teachers' Verbal Behavior." Dissert. Abstr., 1965; 25:3991-92.

Fattu, N. A. "Exploration of Interactions Among Instruction, Content and Aptitude Variables."
J. Teach. Ed., Sept., 1963; 14 (No. 3), 244-50.

Feldhusen, J. F., Thurston, J. R., and Benning, J. J. "Classroom Behavior and School
Achievement: A Longitudinal Study." Paper presented at the American Educational
Research Association convention, New York, February, 1967.

Filson, T. N. "Factors Influencing the Level of Dependence in the Classroom." Unpublished
doctoral dissertation, University of Minnesota, 1957.

Fine, Harold J., and Zimer, Carl N. "A Quantitative Method of Scaling Communication and
Interaction Process." J. Clin. Psych. July, 1956; 12:268-71.

Flanders, Ned A. Subscripting Interaction Analysis Categories, a 22 Category System. Ann
Arbor: University of Michigan, 1966.

——. "Integrating Theory and Practice in Teacher Education." In forty-fourth yearbook of
the Association for Student Teaching, Theoretical Bases for Professional Laboratory
Experiences in Teacher Education. Dubuque, Iowa: Association for Student Teaching,
1965.

——. "Teacher Influence, Pupil Attitudes, and Achievement." United States Department of
Health, Education, and Welfare, Office of Education, Cooperative Research Monograph
No. 12. Washington, D. C.: Government Printing Office, 1965.

——. "Some Relationships Between Teacher Influence, Pupil Attitudes and Achievement."
In B. J. Biddle and W. J. Ellena (Eds.) Contemporary Research on Teacher Effectiveness.
New York: Holt, Rinehart, and Winston. 1964.

——. "Intent, Action and Feedback: A Preparation for Teaching." J. Teach. Ed., 1963;
14:251-260.

——. "Teacher Influence in the Classroom." In Arno Bellack (Ed.) Theory and Research in
Teaching. 1963; 37-52.

——. "Using Interaction Analysis in the Inservice Training of Teachers." J. Exp. Ed.,
30 (No. 4), June, 1962.

——. "Diagnosing and Utilizing Social Structures in Classroom Learning." In Nelson B.
Henry (Ed.) The Dynamics of Instructional Groups. Chicago: N.S.S.E., University of
Chicago Press, 1960. 59th Yearbook. pp. 187-217.

——. "Teacher-Pupil Contacts and Mental Hygiene." J. Soc. Issues, 1959; 15:30-39.

——. "Personal-Social Anxiety as a Factor in Experimental Learning Situations."
J. Ed. Res., 1951; 45:100-110.

Flanders, Ned, and Amidon, Edmund. "Two Approaches to the Teaching Process." NEA
Journal, May, 1962, 51:43-45.

Flanders, Ned A., and Havumaki, S. "Group Compliance to Dominative Teacher Influence."
J. Hum. Rel., 1960; 13:67-82.

Flanders, Ned A., and Simon, Anita. "Teacher Effectiveness." In Robert L. Ebel, (Ed.)
Encyclopedia of Educational Research (4th ed.), 1970 (in press).

Fowler, Beverly D. "Relation of Teacher Personality Characteristics and Attitudes to Teacher-Pupil Rapport and Emotional Climate in the Elementary Classroom." Unpublished doctoral dissertation, University of South Carolina, Columbia, 1961.

Furst, Norma. "The Multiple Languages of the Classroom: A Further Analysis and a Synthesis of Meanings Communicated in High School Teaching." Unpublished doctoral dissertation, Temple University, Philadelphia, 1967.

———. "The Effects of Training in Interaction Analysis on the Behavior of Student Teachers in Secondary Schools." Paper presented at the American Educational Research Association meeting, Chicago, February, 1965.

Gage, N. L. "Research on Cognitive Aspects of Teaching." The Way Teaching Is. (Stanford U.) A.S.C.D. and the Center for the Study of Instruction of the NEA. 1966.

———. "Desirable Behaviors of Teachers." Urban Ed., 1965; 1:85-95.

———. "A Method for Improving Teacher Behavior." J. Teach. Ed., 1963; 14:261-66.

Gage, N. L. (Ed.) Handbook of Research on Teaching. New York: Rand McNally, 1963.

Gallagher, James J. "A Topic Classification System in Analysis of BSCS Concept Presentation." In Anita Simon (Ed.) Classroom Interaction Newsletter, Vol. II, No. 2, Philadelphia, May, 1967.

———. "Expressive Thought by Gifted Children in the Classroom." El. Eng., 1965; 42:559-68.

Gallagher, James, et al. "A System of Topic Classification: Classroom Interaction Study." Institute for Research on Exceptional Children. Urbana: University of Illinois, 1966.

Gallagher, J. and Aschner, M. J. "A Preliminary Report on Analysis of Classroom Interaction." Merril-Palmer Quarterly, 1963.

Galloway, Charles. "An Exploratory Study of Observational Procedures for Determining Teacher Nonverbal Communication." Unpublished doctoral dissertation, University of Florida, Gainesville, 1962.

Giammatteo, Michael C. "Interaction Patterns of Elementary Teachers Using the Minnesota Categories for Interaction Analysis." Doctoral dissertation, University of Pittsburgh, 1963.

Gibb, Cecil A. "Classroom Behavior of the College Teacher." J. Ed. and Psychol. Meas. August, 1955; 15:254-63.

Gilstrap, Robert. The Teacher in Action, A Guide for Student Observers in Elementary School Classroom. Adapted from the Provo Code for the Analysis of Teaching. Provo, Utah: Provo City Schools Research Staff, 1961.

Gnagey, William J. "Effects on Classmates of a Deviant Student's Power and Response to a Teacher-Exerted Control Technique." J. Ed. Psychol., February, 1960; 51:1-8.

Gordon, C. W. The Social System of the High School. Illinois: The Free Press, 1957.

Gordon, C. W. and McNeil, J. D. "Teacher Leadership Styles in Relation to Productivity, Morale, and Achievement Among Seventh and Eighth Grade Pupils." Cooperative Research Project No. 1084, September, 1960 - February, 1962.

Gordon, W. J. J. Synectics: The Development of Creative Capacity. New York: Harper and Brothers. 1961.

Gotts, Edward E., Adams, Russell L., and Phillips, Beeman N. "A Classification System for Discrete Pupil Behaviors." Paper presented at the American Educational Research Association convention, New York, February, 1967.

Guggenheim, P. "Classroom Climate and the Learning of Mathematics." Arith. Teach., 1961; 8:363-7.

Guilford, J. P., Christensen, P. R., Taafee, G. and Wilson, R. C. "Ratings Should be Scrutinized." Ed. and Psych. Meas., 1962; 22 (No. 3).

Guszak, Frank J. "Reading Comprehension Development as Viewed from the Standpoint of Teacher Questioning Strategies." Paper presented at the American Educational Research Association convention, New York, February, 1967.

Hall, D. M. Dynamics of Group Action. Danville, Illinois: The Interstate Printers and Publishers, Inc., 1957.

Hanny, Robert Joseph. "The Relationship Between Selected Personality Characteristics and Teacher Verbal Behavior." Unpublished doctoral dissertation, Ohio State University, Columbus, 1966.

Harrington, G. M. "Smiling as a Measure of Teacher Effectiveness." J. Ed. Res., 1955; 48:715-17.

Harvey, O. H., Prather, M., White, J. B., and Hoffmeister, J. K. "Teachers' Beliefs, Classroom Atmosphere, and Student Behavior." Paper presented at the American Educational Research Association convention, New York, February, 1967.

Hayes, Robert B., Keim, Floyd N. and Neiman, Albert M. "The Effects of Student Reactions to Teaching Methods." Bureau of Research Administration and Coordination, Department of Public Instruction, Harrisburg, Penna. Cooperative Research Project No. 6-2056, September, 1967.

Heil, L. M., Powell, M. and Feifer, I. "Characteristics of Teacher Behavior and Competency Related to the Achievement of Different Kinds of Children in Several Elementary Grades." Cooperative Research Project SA E 7285, 1960.

Heil, L. M., and Washburne, C. "Brooklyn College Research in Teacher Effectiveness." J. Ed. Res., 1962; 55:347-51.

———. "Characteristics of Teachers Related to Children's Progress." J. Teach. Ed., 1961; 12:401-6.

Herbert, John. "The Analysis of Lessons." In Anita Simon (Ed.) Classroom Interaction Newsletter, Vol. II, No. 1, Philadelphia, November, 1966.

Herman, Wayne Leroy, Jr. "An Analysis of the Activities and Verbal Behavior of Selected Fifth Grade Social Studies Classes." In Anita Simon (Ed.) Classroom Interaction Newsletter, Vol. II, No. 2, Philadelphia, May, 1967.

Heyns, R. W., and Lippett, R. "Systematic Observational Techniques." In G. Lindzey (Ed.) Handbook of Social Psychology. Cambridge: Addison-Wesley Publishing Co., 1954, p. 370-404.

Heyns, R. W., and Zander, A. F. "Observation of Group Behavior." In L. Festinger and D. Katz (Eds.) Research Methods in the Behavioral Sciences. New York: Dryden, 1953; pp. 381-417.

Hill, William Morris. "The Effects on Verbal Teaching Behavior of Learning Interaction as an In-Service Education Activity." Unpublished doctoral dissertation, Ohio State University, Columbus, 1966.

Hirschi, Edwin and Meux, Milton O. "A Comparison of a Discovery Teaching Strategy and a Traditional Discussion Strategy." Paper presented at the American Educational Research Association convention, New York, February, 1967.

Honigman, Fred K. MACI Abstract. Philadelphia: Department of Curriculum and Instruction, School District of Philadelphia, 1967.

———. Multidimensional Analysis of Classroom Interaction (MACI). Villanova, Pennsylvania: The Villanova University Press, 1967.

———. "Testing a Three Dimensional System for Analyzing Teacher Influence." Unpublished doctoral dissertation, Temple University, Philadelphia, 1966.

Hoover, N. H. "Degree of Teacher Domination in Group Processes and Student Attitude Toward Instruction in Secondary Methods Classes." J. Ed. Res., 1963; S6:379-81.

Hough, John B. "Training in the Control of Verbal Teaching Behavior — Theory and Implications." Paper presented at the American Educational Research Association convention, New York, February, 1967.

———. "An Observational System for the Analysis of Classroom Instruction." In Edmund J. Amidon and John B. Hough (Eds.) Interaction Analysis: Theory, Research and Application. Reading, Mass: Addison-Wesley Publishing Co., 1967, pp. 150-7.

———. "Classroom Interaction and the Facilitation of Learning: The Source of an Instructional Theory." ibid. pp. 375-87.

———. "Interaction Analysis in a General Methods Course." In Anita Simon (Ed.) Classroom Interaction Newsletter, Vol. I, No. 2, Philadelphia, May, 1966.

———. "A Study of the Effect of Five Experimental Treatments on the Development of Human Relations Skills and Verbal Teaching Behaviors of Pre-Service Teachers." Unpublished paper (mimeographed copies available from the author). College of Education, Ohio State University, Columbus, 1965.

———. "The Dogmatism Factor in the Human Relations Training of Pre-Service Teachers." Paper presented at the annual meeting of the American Educational Research Association, Chicago, 1965.

Hough, John B., and Amidon, Edmund J. "The Relationship of Personality Structure and Training in Interaction Analysis to Attitude Change During Student Teaching." Paper presented at the annual meeting of the American Educational Research Association, Chicago, 1965.

——. "An Experiment in Pre-Service Teacher Education." ibid. 1964.

——. "Behavioral Change in Pre-Service Teacher Preparation: An Experimental Study." College of Education, Temple University, Philadelphia, 1964.

Hough, John B., and Duncan, J. K. "Exploratory Studies of a Teaching Situation Reaction Test." Paper presented at the annual meeting of the American Educational Research Association, Chicago, 1965.

Hough, John B., and Ober, R. "The Effects of Training in Interaction Analysis on the Verbal Behavior of Pre-Service Teachers." Paper presented at the annual meeting of the American Educational Research Association, Chicago, 1966.

Howsam, R. B. "Who's a Good Teacher: Problems and Progress in Teacher Evaluation." Prepared for the Joint Committee on Personnel Procedures of the California School Board Assn. and the California Teachers Assn., California Teachers Assn., 1960, 48 p.

Hughes, Marie. "What is Teaching? One Viewpoint." Ed. Lead., June, 1962; 19:251-9.

——. "Patterns of Effective Teaching." Second Progress Report of the Merit Study of the Provo City Schools, June, 1961.

——. "Development of the Means for the Assessment of the Quality of Teaching in Elementary Schools." USOE Cooperative Research Project No. 353, University of Utah, Salt Lake City, 1959.

——. Helping Students Understand Teaching. Salt Lake City: University of Utah, 1959.

Hughes, Marie, et al. "The Assessment of the Quality of Teaching: A Research Report." U. S. Office of Education, Cooperative Research Project No. 353, University of Utah, Salt Lake City, 1959.

Hunkins, Francis P. "The Influence of Analysis and Evaluation Questions on Achievement in Sixth Grade Social Studies." Paper presented at the American Educational Research Association convention, New York, February, 1967.

——. "The Questions Asked: Effectiveness of Inquiry Techniques in Elementary School Social Studies." ibid.

Jackson, P. "The Way Teaching Is." A. S. C. D. and The Center for the Study of Instruction of the NEA, 1966.

Johns, Joseph P. "The Relationship Between Teacher Behavior and the Incidence of Thought-Provoking Questions by Students in Secondary Schools." Unpublished doctoral dissertation, University of Michigan, Anne Arbor, 1966. 103 p.

Johnson, Mauritz, Jr. "Junior High School Research Series: Junior High School Project." School of Education, Cornell University, Ithaca, New York, April, 1965.

Jones, L. H. "Student and Teacher Interactions During Evaluative Dialogues in Art." J. of Art Ed., April, 1965; 18:13-15.

Joyce, Bruce R. "Flexibility in Teacher Behavior." In Anita Simon (Ed.) Classroom Interaction Newsletter, Vol. II, No. 2, Philadelphia, May, 1967.

Joyce, Bruce and Harootunian, Berj. The Structure of Teaching. Chicago: Science Research Associates, 1967.

Joyce, Bruce R., and Hodges, Richard E. "Instructional Flexibility Training." J. Teach. Ed., Winter, 1966; 17 (No. 4), 409-15.

——. "A Rationale for Teacher Education." El. Sch. J., 1966; 66:254-66.

Kirk, Jeffery. "Effects of Teaching the Minnesota System of Interaction Analysis to Intermediate Grade Student Teachers." Unpublished doctoral dissertation, Temple University, Philadelphia, 1963.

Kliebard, H. M. "Teacher Cycles: A Study of the Pattern and Flow of Classroom Discourse." Doctor of Ed. Project Report, Teachers College, Columbia University, New York, 1963.

Komisar, B. Paul. "Questions for Research on Teaching." In Anita Simon (Ed.) Classroom Interaction Newsletter, Vol. III, No. 1, Philadelphia, December, 1967.

Kounin, Jacob S. "Observation and Analysis of Classroom Management." Paper presented at the American Educational Research Association convention, New York, February, 1967.

Krathwohl, D., Bloom, B. and Masia, B. Taxonomy of Educational Objectives II: Affective Domain. New York: David McKay Co., 1964.

LaGrone, Herbert F. "A Proposal for the Revision of the Pre-Service Professional Component of a Program of Teacher Education." U. S. Dept. of Health, Education, and Welfare, Office of Education, Educational Media Branch, Contract No. OE3-16-006. Washington, D.C.: American Association of Colleges for Teacher Education, 1964.

Lambert, Philip. "Classroom Interaction, Pupil Achievement, and Adjustment in Team Teaching as Compared with the Self-Contained Classroom." Cooperative Research Project No. 1391, 1961-1964.

Lambert, P. and others. "Comparison of Pupil Achievement in Team and Self-Contained Organizations." J. Exp. Ed., Spring, 1965; 33:217-24.

LaShier, William S., Jr. "An Analysis of Certain Aspects of the Verbal Behavior of Student Teachers of Eighth Grade Students Participating in a BSCS Laboratory Block." Unpublished doctoral dissertation, University of Texas, Austin, 1965.

Lawler, E. S. "Differing Rates of Progress of Classes Under the Same and Different Teachers." J. Ed. Res., 1964; 58:84-6.

Leurs, W. W., and Newell, J. M. "Analysis of Classroom Interaction Through Communication Behaviors." J. Exp. Ed., June, 1962; 30 (No. 4), 321-22.

Levin, Harry, Hilton, Thomas, and Leiderman, Gloria. "Studies of Teacher Behavior." J. Exp. Ed., September, 1957; 26:81-91.

Lewin, K., et al. Changing Behavior and Attitudes. Cambridge: Massachusetts Institute of Technology, 1945.

Lewin, K. "Field Theory and Experiment in Social Psychology." Amer. J. Soc., 1939; 44:868-896.

Lewin, I. Dynamic Theory of Personality. New York: McGraw-Hill, 1935.

Lewin, K., Lippitt, R., and White, R. "Patterns of Aggressive Behavior in Experimentally Created Social Climates." J. Soc. Psychol., May, 1939; 10:271-99.

Lewis, W., Newell, J., and Withall, J. "An Analysis of Classroom Patterns of Communication." Psychol. Rep., 1961; 9:211-19.

Lewis, W. W., Withall, J., and Newell, J. M. "A Description of Two Instructional Approaches." Mental Health Teacher Education Research Project, Madison: University of Wisconsin, 1960.

Lieberman, G. F., Hilton, T. L., and Levin, H. "Studies of Teacher's Behavior: A Summary Report." J. Teach. Ed., 1957; 8:433-37.

Lindvall, C. M. "The Role of Classroom Observation in the Improvement of Instruction." In Anita Simon (Ed.) Classroom Interaction Newsletter, Vol. III, No. 1, Philadelphia, December, 1967.

Lindvall, C. M., et al. Manual for IPI Student Observational Form. Unpublished document, Learning Research and Development Center, University of Pittsburgh, Undated, (mimeo.).

Lippitt, R. "An Analysis of Group Reaction to three Types of Experimentally Created Social Climates." Unpublished doctoral dissertation, University of Iowa, Iowa City, 1940.

———. "An Experimental Study of Authoritarian and Democratic Group Atmospheres." Stud. Child Welfare, 1940; 16:43-195.

Lohman, Ernest E. "Differential Effects of Training on the Verbal Behavior of Student Teachers — Theory and Implications." Paper presented at the American Educational Research Association convention, New York, February, 1967.

McDonald, James B., and Zaret, Esther. "Report of a Study of Openness in Classroom Interactions." Paper presented at the American Educational Research Association convention, New York, February, 1967.

Maier, Norman, and Maier, Richard. "An Experimental Test of the Effects of 'Development' vs. 'Free' Discussion on the Quality of Group Decisions." J. Applied Psychol., October, 1957; 320-23.

Mastin, Victor E. "Teacher Enthusiasm." J. Ed. Res., March, 1963; 56:385-86.

McDonald, F. J. "Applying the Language of Behavioral Models to Teaching Acts." Paper presented at the American Educational Research Association convention, New York, February, 1967.

McKeachie, W. J. "Research on Teaching at the College and University Level." In N. L. Gage (Ed.) Handbook of Research on Teaching. Chicago: Rand McNally, 1963.

McNaughton, A. H., Crawford, W. R., Ho, Shu-Kie, and Wallen, N. E., "The Use of Teaching Modules to Study High Level Thinking in the Social Studies." Paper presented at the American Educational Research Association convention, New York, February, 1967.

Medley, Donald, "Experiences with the OScAR Technique." J. Teach. Ed., September, 1963; 14 (No. 3), 267-73.

——. "Teacher Personality and Teacher-Pupil Rapport." J. Teach. Ed., 1961; 12:152-6.

Medley, Donald, and Hill, Russell. "OScAR at Temple." In Anita Simon (Ed.) Classroom Interaction Newsletter, Vol. II, No. 1, Philadelphia, November, 1966.

Medley, Donald M., Impellitteri, Joseph T., Smith, Lou, H. "Coding Teachers' Verbal Behavior in the Classroom, A Manual for Users of OScAR 4V." From A Report of the Office of Research and Evaluation, Division of Teacher Education of the City University of New York, Undated.

Medley, D. M., and Klein, A. A. "Measuring Classroom Behavior with a Pupil-Reaction Inventory." El. Sc. J., March, 1957; 57:315-19.

Medley, Donald M., and Mitzel, Harold E. "A Tentative Framework for the Study of Effective Teacher Behavior." J. Exp. Ed., June, 1962; 30 (No. 4): 317-20.

——. "Some Behavioral Correlates of Teacher Effectiveness." J. Ed. Psychol., 1959; 50:239-246.

——. "Application of Analysis of Variance to the Estimation of the Reliability of Observations of Teachers' Classroom Behavior." J. Exp. Ed., September, 1958; Vol. 27.

——. "Technique for Measuring Classroom Behavior." J. Ed. Psychol., 1958; 49:86-92.

——. Studies of Teacher's Behavior: Refinement of Two Techniques for Assessing Teacher's Classroom Behavior. New York: Division of Teacher Education, 1955.

Meyer, William, and Thompson, George. "Sex Differences in the Distribution of Teacher Approval and Disapproval Among Sixth-Grade Children." J. Ed. Psychol., November, 1956; 47:385-96.

Miller, George L. "Collaborative Teaching and Pupil Thinking." J. Teach. Ed., 1966; 17 (No. 3).

——. The Collaboration Scale for the Analysis of Teaching: Responsive-Directive Dimension. Lesley College, Cambridge, Massachusetts, April, 1966. (Mimeo.).

——. "An Investigation of Teaching Behavior and Pupil Thinking." Department of Education, University of Utah, Salt Lake City, 1964.

Mitzel, Harold E. "Teacher Effectiveness." In Chester W. Harris (Ed.) Encyclopedia of Educational Research (3rd Ed.). New York: Macmillan, 1960. p. 1481-86.

——. "A Behavioral Approach to the Assessment of Teacher Effectiveness." Paper, New York City College of Education, New York, 1957.

Mitzel, Harold E., and Gross, Cecily. "The Development of Pupil Growth Criteria in Studies of Teacher Effectiveness." Ed. Res. Bulletin, 1958; Vol. 37.

Mitzel, Harold E., and Medley, Donald. "Pupil-Growth in Reading — An Index of Effective Teaching." J. Ed. Psychol., April, 1957; 48:227-39.

Mitzel, Harold E., and Rabinowitz, W. "Assessing Social-Emotional Climate in the Classroom by Withall's Technique." Psych. Monogr., American Psychological Association, Washington, D.C.: 1953; 67 (No. 18).

Molchen, Kenneth J. "A Study of Changes in the Intentions, Perceptions, and Classroom Verbal Behavior of Science Interns and Apprentices." In Anita Simon (Ed.) Classroom Interaction Newsletter, Vol. II, No. 1, Philadelphia, May, 1967.

——. "Intentions, Perceptions, and Classroom Verbal Behavior." Paper presented at the American Educational Research Association convention, New York, February, 1967.

Morgan, Jack Collins. "A Study of the Observed Behaviors of Student Teachers in Secondary Social Studies as Correlates with Certain Personality Characteristics and Creativity." In Anita Simon (Ed.) Classroom Interaction Newsletter, Vol. II, No. 2, Philadelphia, May, 1967.

Morrison, B. M. "The Reactions of Internal and External Children to Patterns of Teaching Behavior." Unpublished doctoral dissertation, University of Michigan, Ann Arbor, 1966.

Morrison, Virginia Bailey. "Teacher Pupil Interaction in Elementary Urban Schools." In Anita Simon (Ed.) Classroom Interaction Newsletter, Vol. II, No. 1, Philadelphia, November, 1966.

——. "The Relationship of Student Teacher Performance and Pupil Performance to Supervisory and Pupil Merit Ratings." Doctoral dissertation, University of Michigan, Ann Arbor, 1961.

Morse, William, et al. A Study of School Classroom Behavior from Diverse Evaluative Frameworks: Developmental, Mental Health, Substantive Learning, and Group Process. Cooperative Research Project No. 753, 1961.

Morsh, J. E. "Developmental Report - Systematic Observation of Instructor Behavior." Res. Bulletin A.F.P.T.R.C. - TN-56-52, U. S. Air Force, 1956.

Morsh, J. E., and Wilder, E. M. "Identifying the Effective Instructor: A Review of Quantitative Studies, 1900-1952." Research Bulletin No. AFPTRC-TR-54-44, USAF Personnel Training Research Center, San Antonio, Texas, 1954.

Moskowitz, Gertrude. "The Effect of Training in Interaction Analysis on the Attitudes and Teaching Patterns of Cooperating Teachers and their Student Teachers." Unpublished doctoral dissertation, Temple University, Philadelphia, 1966.

——. "The FLint System: An Observational Tool for the Foreign Language Class (Foreign Language Interaction System)." Unpublished document (mimeo), College of Education, Temple University, Philadelphia, 1966.

Moustakas, Clark, Sigel, Irving, and Schalock, Henry. "An Objective Method of the Measurement and Analysis of Child-Adult Interaction." Child. Devel., June, 1956; 27:109-34.

Nelson, Lois Ney. "Teacher Leadership: An Empirical Approach to Analyzing Teacher Behavior in the Classroom." In Anita Simon (Ed.) Classroom Interaction Newsletter, Vol. II, No. 1, Philadelphia, November, 1966.

——. "The Effect of Classroom Interaction on Pupil Linguistic Performance." Dissert. Abstr., 1964; 25:1789.

Nuthall, Graham. "University of Illinois Project on the Strategies of Teaching." In Anita Simon (Ed.) Classroom Interaction Newsletter, Vol. II, No. 1, Philadelphia, November, 1966.

Ober, Richard L. "Predicting the Verbal Behavior of Student Teachers." Paper presented at the American Educational Research Association convention, New York, February, 1967.

——. "Predicting Student Teacher Verbal Behavior." Unpublished doctoral dissertation, Ohio State University, Columbus, 1966.

Ohnmacht, Fred W. "Relationships Among Field Independence, Dogmatism, Teacher Characteristics and Teaching Behavior of Pre-Service Teachers." Paper presented at the American Educational Research Association convention, New York, February, 1967.

Oliver, D. W., and Shaver, J. P. "The Development of a Multi-Dimensional Observation System for the Analysis of Pupil-Teacher Interaction." Paper presented at the American Educational Research Association convention, Chicago, 1963.

——. "The Use of Content Analysis of Oral Discussions as a Method of Evaluating Political Education." ibid.

——. The Analysis of Public Controversy; A Study in Citizenship Education. Cambridge, Mass.: Harvard Graduate School of Education, 1962.

Olson, W. C., et al. "Teacher Personality as Revealed by the Amount and Kind of Verbal Direction used in Behavior Control." Educ. Admin. Superv., 1938; 24:81-93.

Openshaw, M. Karl and Cyphert, Frederick R. The Development of a Taxonomy for the Classification of Teacher Classroom Behavior. Ohio State University Research Foundation, 1966.

Pankratz, Roger. "Verbal Interaction Patterns in the Classroom of Selected Physics Teachers." In Edmund J. Amidon and John B. Hough (Eds.) Interaction Analysis: Theory Research and Application. Reading, Mass: Addison-Wesley Publishing Company, 1967, pp. 189-210.

Parakh, J. S. "To Develop a System for Analyzing the Reactions of Teachers and Students in Biology Classes." USOE Cooperative Research Project No. S-269, Cornell University, Ithaca, New York, 1965.

Perkins, Hugh. "Climate Influences Group Learning." J. Educ. Res., 1951; 45:115-119.

——. "The Effects of Social-Emotional Climate and Curriculum on Group Learning of In-Service Teachers." Doctoral dissertation, University of Chicago, Chicago, 1949.

——. "Classroom Behavior and Underachievement." Am. Ed. Res. J., 1965; 2:1-12.

Perkins, Hugh. "A Procedure for Assessing the Classroom Behavior of Students and Teachers." ibid. 1964; 50:240-60.

Pfeiffer, Isobel L. "Comparison of Verbal Interaction and Goals of Teachers Teaching Classes of Different Ability in Eleventh Grade English." Unpublished doctoral dissertation, Kent State University, Kent, Ohio, 1966.

Popham, W. J. "Modifying the Instructional Behavior of Student Teachers." Paper presented at the American Educational Research Association convention, Chicago, 1964.

Powell, Evan R. "Teacher Behavior and Pupil Achievement." Unpublished doctoral dissertation, Temple University, Philadelphia, 1968.

Proctor, Virginia. "A Further Refinement of the Wright Observational Schedule." Masters thesis, Washington University, St. Louis, 1960.

Provo City Schools. Patterns of Effective Teaching. Second Progress Report of the Merit Study of the Provo Schools. Provo, Utah: Provo City Schools, 1961.

Puckett, R. C. "Making Supervision Objective." Sch. Rev., 1928; 36:209-12.

Reed, H. B. "Implications for Science Education of a Teacher Competence Research." Sci. Ed., 1962; 46:473-86.

Reed, H. B. "Effects of Teacher Warmth." J. Teach. Ed., 1961; 12:330-4.

Remmers, H. H. "Rating Methods in Research on Teaching." In N. L. Gage (Ed.) Handbook of Research on Teaching, New York: Rand McNally, 1963; pp. 329-373.

Reynolds, Richard J. "Relationships of Cognitive Complexity to Specific Behavioral Variables." Unpublished doctoral dissertation, State University of New York, Albany, August, 1967.

Ringness, Thomas A. "Effect of Clinical Evaluation on Supervision of Student Teachers." In Anita Simon (Ed.) Classroom Interaction Newsletter, Vol. II, No. 2, Philadelphia, May, 1967.

——. "The Effects of Supervisor Knowledge of Student-Teacher Personality." Paper presented at the Association for the Supervision of Curriculum Development, Curriculum Research Institute, Washington, D. C., 1965.

Ringness, et al. "Self-Role Conflict, Personality Variables, and Classroom Interaction." Extension Research and Services in Education, the University of Wisconsin, Madison, 1964.

Ringness, T. A., and Larson, E. A. "Effect of Clinical Evaluation on Supervision of Student Teachers." University of Wisconsin, Madison, U. S. Office of Education, Project S-194, November, 1965.

Roberts, William L. "Modes of Communicating in Teacher-Student Dialogue." In Anita Simon (Ed.) Classroom Interaction Newsletter, Vol. II, No. 1, Philadelphia, May, 1967.

Rogers, Carl R. "Learning to be Free." In Seymour M. and Roger H. L. Wilson, (Eds.) Conflict and Creativity, New York: McGraw-Hill, 1963.

Rokeach, M. The Open and Closed Mind. New York: Basic Books, 1960.

Romney, G. P., et al. Patterns of Effective Teaching: Second Progress Report of the Merit Study of the Provo City Schools. Provo, Utah, 1961.

——. Progress Report of the Merit Study of the Provo City Schools. Provo, Utah, 1958.

Romoser, R. C. "Change in Attitude and Perception in Teacher Education Students Associated with Instruction in Interaction Analysis." Dissert. Abstr., 1965; 25:5770.

Rose, Gale W. "Performance Evaluation and Growth in Teaching." Phi Delta Kappa, October, 1963; pp. 48-53.

Rowan, Naoma Tew. "The Relationship of Teacher Interaction in Classroom Situations to Teacher Personality Variables." In Anita Simon (Ed.) Classroom Interaction Newsletter, Vol. III, No. 1, Philadelphia, December, 1967.

Ryans, David G. "Teacher Behavior Theory and Research: Implications for Teacher Education." J. Teach. Ed., 1963; 14:274-93.

——. "Inventory Estimated Teacher Characteristics as Covariants of Observer Assessed Pupil Behavior." J. Ed. Psychol., 1961; 52:91-97.

——. "Some Relationships between Pupil Behavior and Certain Teacher Characteristics." ibid., 52:82-90.

——. Characteristics of Teachers: Their Description, Comparison and Appraisal. Washington, D. C.: American Council on Education, 1960.

——. "Prediction of Teacher Effectiveness." In Chester W. Harris (Ed.) Encyclopedia of Educational Research. New York: Macmillan Co., 1960; pp. 1486-91.

——. "Theory Development and the Study of Teacher Behavior." J. Ed. Psychol., 1949; 57:169-75.

Ryans, D. G. and Wandt, E. "A Factor Analysis of Observed Teacher Behavior in the Secondary School." Ed. and Psychol. Meas., 1952; 12:574-86.

Schalock, H. Del. "Issues in the Conceptualization and Measurement of Teaching Behavior." Paper presented at the annual meeting of the American Educational Research Association, New York, February, 1967.

Schantz, Betty Marie Baird. "An Experimental Study Comparing the Effects of Verbal Recall by Children in Direct and Indirect Teaching Methods as a Tool of Measurement." Doctoral dissertation, Pennsylvania State University, University Park, 1963.

Schueler, Herbert, Gold, Milton J., and Mitzel, Harold E. The Use of Television for Improving Teacher Training and for Improving Measures of Student-Teaching Performance. Phase I: Improvement of Student Teaching. U. S. Department of Health, Education, and Welfare, Office of Education, Grant No. 730035. New York: Hunter College, University of New York, 1962.

Scott, W. A. "Reliability of Content Analysis: The Case of Nominal Coding." Publ. Quart., July, 1955; 19:321-25.

Sears, Pauline. "The Effect of Classroom Conditions on the Strength of Self-Esteem, Achievement Motivation and Work Output of Elementary School Children." Cooperative Research Project N. 873, 1960-1962.

———. "What Happens to Pupils Within the Classroom of Elementary Schools." Paper presented at the American Educational Research Association convention, Los Angeles, 1960.

Shapiro, Edna. "Study of Children Through Observation of Classroom Behavior." In Arno Bellack (Ed.) Theory and Research in Teaching, 1963; pp. 91-101.

Shaver, James P. "A Dual Role for Systematic Observation: A Review of Research." In Anita Simon (Ed.) Classroom Interaction Newsletter, Vol. II, No. 1, Philadelphia, November, 1966.

Shaver, James. "A Study of Teaching Style: The Investigation Through Systematic Observation of the Ability of Experimental Teachers to Conform to Two Models of Teaching." Doctoral dissertation, Harvard Graduate School of Education, Cambridge, 1961.

Silberman, H. F. "Studies of Teacher Behavior: Effects of Praise and Reproof on Reading Growth in a Non-Laboratory Classroom Setting." J. Ed. Psych., 1957; 48:199-206.

Simon, Anita. "The Effects of Training in Interaction Analysis on the Teaching Patterns of Student Teachers in Favored and Non-Favored Classes." Unpublished doctoral dissertation, Temple University, Philadelphia, 1966.

Simon, Anita, and others. "Programming Pupil-Teacher Interaction." Paper presented at the American Educational Research Association convention, Chicago, February, 1966.

Simon, Anita (Ed.) Classroom Interaction Newsletter, Vols. I-III, 1965-67, Philadelphia: Temple University.

Simon, Anita, and Agazarian, Yvonne. Sequential Analysis of Verbal Interaction. Philadelphia: Research for Better Schools, Inc., 1967.

———. "Sequential Analysis of Verbal Interaction, Applications I." Part III of a series of three papers presented at the annual convention of the American Association of Humanistic Psychology, New York, September, 1966.

Smith, B. O. "Conceptual Frameworks for Analysis of Classroom Social Interaction." J. Exp. Ed., June, 1962; 30 (No. 4) 325-26.

Smith, B. O., and others. A Tentative Report on the Strategies of Teaching. U. S. Department of Health, Education, and Welfare, Office of Education, Cooperative Research Project No. 1640. Urbana: University of Illinois, 1964.

Smith, B. O., Aschner, M. J., and Meux, M. A Study of the Logic of Teaching. Urbana: University of Illinois, 1962.

Smith, B. O., and Ennis, R. H. Language and Concepts in Education. Chicago: Rand, McNally, 1961.

Smith, L. M. and Lutz, F. W. "Teacher Leader Behavior and Pupil Respect and Liking." J. Ed. Res., 1962.

Smith, M. B. "Interpersonal Relationships in the Classroom Based on the Expected Socioeconomic Status of Sixth Grade Boys." Teach. Col. J., 1965; 36:200-6.

Snider, Ray M. "A Project to Study the Nature of Effective Physics Teaching." USOE Cooperative Research Project No. S-280, Cornell University, Ithaca, New York, 1965.

Soar, Robert S. "Whither Research on Teacher Behavior." In Anita Simon (Ed.) Classroom Interaction Newsletter, Vol. III, No. 1, Philadelphia, December, 1967.

———. "Pupil Growth Over Two Years in Relation to Differences in Classroom Process." Paper presented at the annual meeting of the American Educational Research Association, New York, February, 1967.

———. "Teacher-Pupil Interaction and Pupil Growth." Paper presented at the American Educational Research Association meetings, Chicago, February, 1966.

———. "Pupil Needs and Teacher-Pupil Relationships." Paper presented at the International Reading Association meeting, May, 1965.

———. "Teaching Methods and the Development of Creativity." Paper presented at the American Educational Research Association convention, Chicago, 1965.

———. "Methodological Problems in Predicting Teacher Effectiveness." J. Exp. Ed., 1964; 32:287-91.

———. "An Analysis of Non-Replication in Predicting Teacher Effectiveness." Cooperative Research Project 1170, University of South Carolina, Columbia, 1962.

———. "Multivariate Statistical Procedures in Predicting Teacher-Pupil Classroom Behavior." U. S. Dept. of Health, Education, and Welfare, Office of Education, Cooperative Research Project No. 1170. Columbia: University of South Carolina, 1962.

Solomon, D., et al. "Teacher Behavior and Student Learning." J. Ed. Psychol., 1964; 55:23-30.

Solomon, D., Bexdik, William E. and Rosenberg, Larry. "Dimensions of Teacher Behavior." J. Exp. Ed., 1964; 33 (No. 1) 23-40.

Solomon, Daniel and Miller, Harry. "Exploration in Teaching Styles." Center for the Study of Liberal Education for Adults, 1961.

Sorber, Evan. "Classroom Interaction Patterns and Personality Needs of Traditionally Prepared First Year Elementary Teachers and Graduate Teaching Interns with Degrees from Colleges of Liberal Arts." Doctoral dissertation, University of Pittsburgh, 1964.

Spaulding, Robert L. "A Transactional Approach to Classroom Behavioral Analysis." In Anita Simon (Ed.) Classroom Interaction Newsletter, Vol. III, No. 1, Philadelphia, December, 1967.

———. "Achievement, Creativity, and Self Concept Correlates of Teacher-Pupil Transactions in Elementary Schools." U. S. Department of Health, Education, and Welfare, Office of Education, Cooperative Research Project No. 1352. Urbana: College of Education, University of Illinois, 1963.

Spaulding, R. L. _Affective Dimensions of Creative Processes._ Teacher-Pupil Transactions: University of Illinois, 1963.

——. "Some Correlates of Classroom Teacher Behavior in Elementary Schools." Paper presented at the American Educational Research Association convention, Atlantic City, 1962.

Steinzor, B. "The Development and Evaluation of a Measure of Social Interaction." _Human Relations II_, 1949.

Storlie, T. R. "Selected Characteristics of Teachers Whose Verbal Behavior is Influenced by Inservice Course in Interaction Analysis." Unpublished doctoral dissertation, University of Minnesota, Minneapolis, 1961.

Suchman, J. R. _The Elementary School Training Program in Scientific Inquiry._ Urbana: University of Illinois Press, 1963.

Suchman, J. R. "Inquiry Training: Building Skills for Autonomous Discovery." In W. C. Morse and G. M. Wingo (Eds.) _Psychology and Teaching._ Chicago: Scott Foresman, 1961.

Taba, Hilda. "Patterns and Levels of Thinking in Elementary Class Discussion Sequences." Symposium read at meeting of the American Psychological Association, Philadelphia, August, 1963.

——. "Teaching Strategy and Learning." _Calif. J. Instr. Improv._, December, 1963.

——. _Curriculum Development - Theory and Practice._ New York: Harcourt, Brace and World, 1962.

Taba, Hilda, et al. "Thinking in Elementary School Children," USOE Cooperative Research Project No. 1574. San Francisco State College, 1964.

Thelen, H. A. _Education and the Human Quest._ New York: Harper, 1960.

——. "Experimental Research Toward a Theory of Instruction." _J. Ed. Res._, 1953; 3:212-19.

Thelen, H. A., and Withall, J. G. "Three Forms of Reference: The Description of Climate." _Hum. Rel._, 1949; 2:159-76.

Thomas, Dorothy and others. _Some New Techniques for Studying Social Behavior._ New York: Columbia University, 1929.

Thompson, Glen R. and Bowers, Norman D. "Teaching Style as Related to the Creative Growth of Fourth Grade Children." Paper presented at the annual meeting of the American Educational Research Association, New York, February, 1967.

Travers, Robert M., and others. _Measured Needs of Teachers and Their Behavior in the Classroom._ U. S. Department of Health, Education, and Welfare, Office of Education, Cooperative Research Project No. 444. Salt Lake City: University of Utah, 1961.

Trueblood, Cicil R. "Identifying and then Implementing a Rationale for Teaching." In Anita Simon (Ed.) _Classroom Interaction Newsletter_, Vol. III, No. 1, Philadelphia, December, 1967.

Turner, Richard. "Pupil Influence on Teacher Behavior." In Anita Simon (Ed.) Classroom Interaction Newsletter, Vol. III, No. 1, Philadelphia, December, 1967.

Turner, Richard, and Denny, David. "Teacher Characteristics, Classroom Behavior, and Growth in Pupil Creativity." Paper presented at the annual meeting of the American Educational Research Association, New York, February, 1967.

Turner, R. L. "Task Performance and Teaching Skill in the Intermediate Grades." J. Teach. Ed., September, 1963; 13 (No. 3), 299-307.

Turner, R. L., and Fattu, N. A. "Skill in Teaching, a Reappraisal of the Concepts and Strategies in Teacher Effectiveness Research." Indiana U. Sch. Ed. Bulletin, 1960; 36 (No. 3).

Twelker, Paul A. "Two Types of Teacher-Learner Interaction in Learning by Discovery." Paper presented at the annual meeting of the American Educational Research Association, New York, February, 1967.

Urbach, Floyd D. "A Study of Recurring Patterns of Teaching." Unpublished doctoral dissertation, University of Nebraska, Lincoln, 1966.

Vorreyer, Donald F. "An Analysis of Teacher Classroom Behavior and Role." Dissert. Abstr., March, 1966; 26:5254.

Waimen, Morton D. "Discrimination and Analysis of Teaching Behavior." In Anita Simon (Ed.) Classroom Interaction Newsletter, Vol. I, No. 2, Philadelphia, May, 1966.

——. "Feedback in Classrooms: A Study of Corrective Teacher Responses." J. Exp. Ed., June, 1962; 30 (No. 4), 355-59.

——. "Observing the Classroom Action System." J. Teach. Ed., December, 1961; 12:466-70.

Wallen, Norman E. "Relationships Between Teacher-Characteristics and Student Behavior." Cooperative Research Project 1217, 1961-1963.

Wandt, Edwin, and Ostreicher, Leonard. "Validity of Samples of Classroom Behavior for the Measurement of 'Social-Emotional Climate'." Psychol. Monog., 1954; 68 (No. 4).

Ward, William T. "The Oregon Program." In Anita Simon (Ed.) Classroom Interaction Newsletter, Vol. I, No. 2, Philadelphia, May, 1966.

Webb, Clark, and Baird, J. Hugh. "Learning Differences Resulting from Teacher-and Student-Centered Teaching Methods." Paper presented at the annual meeting of the American Educational Research Association, New York, February, 1967.

Weber, Wilford A. "Teacher and Pupil Creativity." Unpublished doctoral dissertation, Temple University, Philadelphia, 1967.

Whilley, Thomas W. "Student Challenge of Teachers' Teaching." Paper presented at the American Educational Research Association convention, New York, February, 1967.

Wilk, Roger E., and Edson, William H. "Predictions and Performance: An Experimental Study of Student Teachers." J. Teach. Ed., 1963; 14:308-17.

Wilk, Roger E., and Edson, William H.  A Study of the Relationship Between Observed Class-room Behaviors of Elementary Student Teachers, Predictors of Those Behaviors, and Ratings by Supervisors.  U. S. Department of Health, Education, and Welfare, Office of Education, Cooperative Research Project No. 473.  Minneapolis: College of Education, University of Minnesota, 1962.

Willson, Irwin A. "Report of Interaction Analysis Study." In Anita Simon (Ed.) Classroom Interaction Newsletter, Vol. II, No. 2, Philadelphia, May, 1967.

Wise, A. E. "Teacher Influence and Intellectual Initiative in the Classroom." Honors dissertation, Harvard University, Cambridge, 1963.

Withall, John. "Impact on Learners of Climate Created by the Teacher.  Bureau of Audio-Visual Instruction, University of Wisconsin, Madison, 1963.  (FILM).

———. "Mental Health — Teacher Education Research Project." J. Teach. Ed., September, 1963; 14 (No. 3), 318-25.

———. "Research Tools: Observing and Recording Behavior." Rev. Ed. Res., December, 1960; 30:496-512.

———. "Assessment of Social-Emotional Climates Experienced by a Group of Seventh Graders as They Moved from Class to Class." Ed. & Psychol. Meas., 1952; 12:440-45.

———. "The Development of a Climate Index." J. Ed. Rev., 1951; 45:93-99.

———. "The Development of a Technique for the Measurement of Social-Emotional Climate in Classrooms." J. Exp. Ed., 1949; 17:347-61.

Withall, John, and Fagan, John R. "The Effects of an NDEA Institute on the Contents and Verbal Behavior used by English and Reading Teachers to Instruct Disadvantaged Youth." In Anita Simon (Ed.) Classroom Interaction Newsletter, Vol. II, No. 1, Philadelphia, November, 1966.

Withall, John, and Lewis, W. W. "Social Interaction in the Classroom." In N. L. Gage (Ed.) Handbook of Research on Teaching.  New York: Rand, McNally, 1963, pp. 683-714.

Woodruff, Asahel D. "Teacher Education: Current Developments and New Directions." In Anita Simon (Ed.) Classroom Interaction Newsletter, Vol. I, No. 2, Philadelphia, May, 1966.

Wright, E. Muriel J. "Teacher Pupil Interaction in the Mathematics Classroom." Observer's Manual, Appendix No. 1, Technical Report No. 67-5 Minnesota National Laboratory, Minnesota State Department of Education, May, 1967.

———. "Interaction Analysis in the Minnesota National Laboratory Mathematics Field Study." Paper presented at the annual meeting of the American Educational Research Association, New York, February, 1967.

———. "Interaction Analysis to Study Pupil Involvement & Mathematical Content in the Five State Project of the Minnesota National Laboratory." In Anita Simon (Ed.) Classroom Interaction Newsletter, Vol. II, No. 1, Philadelphia, November, 1966.

Wright, E. Muriel J. "A Rationale for Direct Observation of Verbal Education." U. S. Department of Health, Education, and Welfare, Office of Education, Cooperative Research Monograph No. 3, Washington, D. C.: Government Printing Office, 1960.

――――. "A Rationale for Direct Observation of Behaviors in the Mathematics Class." In R. L. Feierabend and P. H. DuBois (Eds.), Psychological Problems and Research Methods in Mathematics Training. St. Louis: Washington University, 1959.

――――. "Development of an Instrument for Studying Verbal Behaviors in a Secondary School Mathematics Classroom." J. Exp. Ed., 1959, No. 28:103-21.

Wright, Muriel, and others. "Patterns and Variability of Verbal Behaviors During Problem Solving in the Typical Subgroups of a High School Geometry Class." Paper presented at the American Educational Research Association convention, 1962.

Wright, Muriel, and Proctor, Virginia. "Systematic Observation of Interaction as a Method of Comparing Mathematics Lessons." Cooperative Research Project No. 816, 1961.

Wrightstone, J. W. Appraisal of Newer Practices in Selected Public Schools. New York: Teachers College, Columbia University, Bureau of Publications, 1935.

――――. "Measuring Teacher Conduct of Class Discussion." El. Sch. J., 1934; 34:454-60.

Zahn, Richard D. "Helping the Beginning Teacher." In Anita Simon (Ed.) Classroom Interaction Newsletter, Vol. II, No. 1, Philadelphia, November, 1966.

――――. "Project Cope Camden Opportunity for Professional Experience." ibid., Vol. I, No. 2, Philadelphia, May, 1966.

――――. "The Use of Interaction Analysis in Supervising Student Teachers." Unpublished doctoral dissertation, Temple University, Philadelphia, 1965.

Zahorik, John A. "The Nature and Value of Teacher Verbal Feedback." Paper presented at the American Educational Research Association convention, New York, February, 1967.

# INDEX TO SYSTEMS AND AUTHORS
## BY SYSTEM NUMBERS

System
Number

Agazarian, Yvonne ............................................................ 18
Amidon, Edmund J. ......................................................... 1, 2
Aschner-Gallagher System ................................................ 3
Aschner, Mary Jane ........................................................ 3
Bellack, Arno .............................................................. 4
Boyer, E. Gil ................................................... Section One
CASES ....................................................................... 21
Collaboration Scale for the Analysis of Teaching:
   Responsive-Directive Dimension ...................................... 14
Conceptual Theory System ............................................... 11
Coping Analysis Schedule for Educational Settings ................ 21
Cyphert, Frederick R. ..................................................... 17
Flanders, Ned A. ......................................................... 5, 6
Flanders System of Interaction Analysis ............................. 5
Flanders (Expanded) ...................................................... 6
Flanders (Sub-categories) ............................................... 6
FLint ........................................................................ 15
Foreign Language Interaction System .................................. 15
Gallagher, James J., et al ............................................. 3, 7
GCS ............................................................. Section One
Generalized Category System ................................. Section One
Honigman, Fred K. .......................................................... 8
Hough, John B. ............................................................. 9
Hughes, Marie M. ...................................................... 10, 14
Hunter, Elizabeth .......................................................... 2
Joyce, Bruce .............................................................. 11
Language of the Classroom, The ........................................ 4
Lindvall, C. M. ........................................................... 12
Logic of Teaching, The .................................................. 19
MACI ......................................................................... 8
MCS .......................................................................... 1
Meux, M. O. ............................................................... 19
Medley, Donald M. ......................................................... 13
Miller, George L. ......................................................... 14
Minnesota National Laboratory Five State System .................. 25
Modified Category System ................................................. 1
Moskowitz, Gertrude ...................................................... 15
Multidimensional Analysis of Classroom Interaction ............... 8
Observational Schedule and Record, Form No. 4, Verbal ........... 13
Observational System for Instructional Analysis ................... 9
Observational System for the Description of Teaching Style ...... 16
Oliver, Donald W. ........................................................ 16
Openshaw, M. Karl ........................................................ 17
OScAR 4V .................................................................. 13
Proctor, Virginia ........................................................ 26
Provo Code for the Analysis of Teaching, The ...................... 10
SAVI ........................................................................ 18

Sequential Analysis of Verbal Interaction ....................................... 18
Shaver, James P. ............................................................. 16
Simon, Anita.................................................... Section One; 18
Smith, B. Othaniel ........................................................ 19, 20
Social-Emotional Climate Index ............................................. 24
Spaulding, Robert L. ...................................................... 21, 22
Spaulding Teacher Activity Rating Schedule ................................... 22
STARS ..................................................................... 22
Strategies of Teaching ...................................................... 20
Student Observational Form - Individually Prescribed Instruction ............... 12
Sub-Categories for Flanders' Ten Category System ........................... 6
Taba, Hilda ............................................................... 23
Taba System ............................................................... 23
Taxonomy of Teacher Behavior ............................................. 17
Topic Classification System ................................................ 7
Verbal Interaction Category System ......................................... 2
VICS ...................................................................... 2
Withall, John .............................................................. 24
Wright, E. Muriel  ....................................................... 25, 26
Wright-Proctor System .................................................... 26